599.74
Lai

Laidler, Keith.
Pandas: giants of the
bamboo forest.

$29.95

c.1

DATE DUE		
DE 3 '94	DEC 2 7 2021	
DE 17 '94		
MY 24 '95		
OC 1 1 '95		
MR 2 '96		
DEC. 19 1998		
NOV. 2 1998		
NOV. 8 1999		
MAR 03 2001		
NOV 3 0 2005		
MAY 1 0 2007		

PANDAS

GIANTS OF THE BAMBOO FOREST

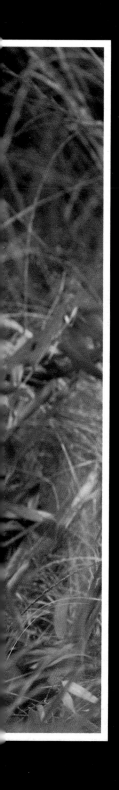

PANDAS

GIANTS OF THE BAMBOO FOREST

———— ••• ————

KEITH AND LIZ LAIDLER

BBC BOOKS

ACKNOWLEDGEMENTS

We could not have written this book without Vera Laidler's stamina in entertaining two demanding toddlers. Our thanks also to all those in CFCC who were involved in the project. Mr Shen Zhihua was especially invaluable in helping to make things run smoothly on location. The project benefited from his patience and administrative diligence, and we also gained a friend. Thanks to, Ms Yan Mingxia and her colleagues at Chengdu Film and Television Foreign Service Company. Our friends at Wolong Giant Panda Nature Reserve were as concerned as ourselves about the programme's successful outcome. They were most supportive in helping us to film, as well as in passing on scientific information. Special thanks to Mr Zhang Hemin, the assistant director, and to Mr Qiu and Mr He, veterinary surgeons.

We are also very grateful to Mr Bob Lewin of Mill Pond Press and Ms Anne Harrel, without whose early help and support the project would probably not have got off the ground.

Julian Flanders, of BBC Enterprises, was thoroughness itself in ensuring the manuscript was presented in an orderly form.

PICTURE CREDITS

All photographs by Keith & Liz Laidler, except: pages 2, 7, 14, 22, 23, 31, 34–5, 42–3, 51, 63, 74–5, 79, 102, 114–15 and 154–5 by Ben Osborne; 143 and 171 Syndication International; 147 Robert Harding Picture Library; 174 (top) WWF/Chris Williott and 174 (bottom) Rex Features/Jo Gipps.

Published by BBC Books,
a division of BBC Enterprises Limited,
Woodlands, 80 Wood Lane, London W12 0TT
First published 1992
The moral right of the authors has been asserted
© Keith and Liz Laidler 1992
ISBN 0 563 36361 4
Designed by Bill Mason
Illustrations by Tony Garrett
Set in 12/15pt Garamond by Butler & Tanner Ltd, Frome
Printed and bound in Great Britain by Butler & Tanner Ltd, Frome

Colour separations by Technik Ltd, Berkhamsted
Jacket printed by Lawrence Allen Ltd,. Weston-super-Mare

CONTENTS

———

*Misty and mysterious – the Mountains of Muping, Père Armand's
'Promised Land'*

INTRODUCTION

The giant panda has the sort of face and lovable appeal that fits well into a child's picture book or a nursery. And if sales of toy pandas are anything to go by, this appeal is universal. In the past twelve months one major toyshop chain in the UK has sold more than 30 000 toy pandas. Total world sales of panda toys have been estimated at over three million per year, with a value of around £10 million. At the same time, the 'original' animal, the blueprint for all those cuddly creatures that our children love to hug, numbers less than 1000 and receives for its protection no more than one tenth of the money spent on its polyester and plastic lookalikes.

Throughout history the giant panda has meant different things to different people. To nineteenth-century taxonomists, it was a mythical creature come to life; and then, a few years later, a trophy to be bagged by hunters and museum collectors. To latter-day Chinese peasants, it was a symbol of good fortune. Today, it symbolises a global conservation ethic. Despite all this attention, the only certain fact on this monochrome creature until recently was its colourful reputation, and the little that was known about its biology could have been written on one of its toyland spin-offs. Its markings have always been admired; its ear markings, eye patches and black vest that continues down its forelegs making it a particularly cuddlesome bear. But that, apart from the fact that it ate bamboo and lived in China, was about as much as most people knew, or cared, about one of the world's most unusual beasts.

In some ways though, the giant panda's popularity today has proved to be a liability. With so many toy pandas around the creature has become a permanent part of our society's traditions, a safe cuddly toy, integral to the cosseted and protected world of our childhood. Given such associations it is small wonder that most of us hardly considered the plight of the real creature in the harsh world outside, and even if we did it was relatively easy to convince ourselves that the giant panda was in no danger. After all, who would want to hurt such a lovely animal?

It came as something of a shock, therefore, when in the mid-1970s reports of a 'natural disaster' started to filter through from a China that was only just beginning to open up to the West. Over vast areas of the giant panda's range its staple food, the bamboo, was dying. In the Qionglai Mountains of western Sichuan Province, at Wolong, a population of more than 150 giant pandas in 1969 had been reduced to just 20 by 1980.

But the bamboo die-back proved a blessing in disguise, and a strange fact emerged from emergency studies carried out by the Chinese. In localities where one or more bamboo species did not flower, panda mortality was negligible, but where flowering occurred in the only species present mortality was to be extremely high. And habitats with only a single bamboo species were almost invariably degraded by human occupation and interference. The lesson was obvious – the giant panda had been in danger long before the emergency of the mid-70s, a victim not of bamboo die-back, but of habitat loss. The expansion of the human population and its inherent pressure on agricultural land had long denied the pandas' food sources and the ability to migrate from one area to another in search of an alternative.

Bamboo die-back had a second benefit; it was realised that science knew next to nothing about the biology of the giant panda, or its smaller cousin, the red panda. Social behaviour, movement patterns, activity cycles during the seasons – information vital to the management of both species – was entirely lacking. Without such facts it was all but impossible to devise a workable management plan to save the pandas. In 1980, following a 1974–77 census of giant pandas throughout China, work began in earnest in the Wolong Valley. A research centre was built and field studies began. Later, attempts were made to study giant pandas breeding in captivity, with a view to supplementing the wild population with captive-bred animals. Since this pioneering effort, several more studies have been initiated in different regions, with both the red and giant pandas coming under scrutiny.

This book details the results of all these studies. Much has now been learned about the behaviour and needs of both species of panda. A comprehensive management plan has now been devised that may save the giant panda (and possibly the red panda too) from extinction. But *may* is the operative word, since recent computer statistics predict the demise of the pandas in the wild within the next few decades. These years are crucial to panda survival. If the management plan fails, it is more than likely that the only panda that our grandchildren will ever know will be the one tucked up in bed with them at night.

The giant panda's unique black and white patterning has so far defied explanation

CHAPTER 1

HOME OF THE PANDAS

China is the only natural home of the giant panda. This creature of fame and fable lives in the mountains of three adjoining provinces: Gansu and Shaanxi in the north and China's biggest and most populous province, Sichuan, in the west of China proper. The red panda shares much of the giant panda's range and is also found in Yunnan Province and the south-eastern corner of Tibet. Its range outside China extends to northern India, Nepal, Sikkim, Bhutan and northern Burma.

Sichuan, 'land of the clouds', is by far the biggest of the three panda provinces, and the most interesting, geologically as well as biologically. It is a magical place, shrouded in mist and mystery. Many strange animals and plants are found only here, evolutionary products of an area insulated from past geological and climatic upheavals by an almost complete ring of mountains. These mountains are ancient beyond telling. They have witnessed the rise and fall of many mountain ranges during geological time, including the world's loftiest, the Himalayas. By Sichuan's standards, the Himalayas are adolescents, created a mere fifty million years ago when the Indian subcontinent collided with the East Asian landmass and caused the earth to buckle and rise up. Remaining largely unperturbed throughout this momentous event, and cut off from outside gene pools, Sichuan became the breeding ground of numerous species found nowhere else on earth.

During the last Ice Age, Sichuan's ring of mountains also acted as a rampart that prevented the advance of the vast southbound glaciers. The land within was a welcome refuge against the ice. Many species that were once widespread across Eurasia thrived within the protective flanks of the mountains and mingled with an exciting array of endemic species. That much of this diversity survives today in China's most populous province is due to the fact that the peaks are too cold and steep for agriculture.

Standing around 1 m (about 3 ft) tall at the shoulders and weighing up to 100 kg (220 lbs), the giant panda is known in China as the 'large cat-bear', an apt title as it combines the soft features of a cat with the profile and body-shape of a bear. Equally bear-like is its habit of sitting upright to feed. Its muzzle is considerably more flattened than a bear's, however, and its ears are short and rounded. The giant panda's black and white markings make it one of the most distinctive of mammals: black ears and eyespots, with a black stole around its shoulders that extends down to its forepaws, and matching black leggings. Its white tail is short and, like the white on its back and belly, is quite often a soiled cream colour. Giant panda fur is thick and covered in an oil that prevents it from getting wet in the permanently soggy atmosphere of its mountain home. A panda's forepaws are equipped with an additional 'thumb' that is used to manipulate the bamboo that forms the panda's staple diet.

The red panda looks more like a racoon than a bear. It is only one-twentieth the weight of a giant panda and a quarter its height at the shoulder. Its thick banded tail, pointed ears and masked face closely resemble those of the racoon, and the 'foxy' muzzle and almost incandescent russet fur have earned it the Chinese name of 'firefox'. Unlike the giant panda it does not lie or sit to eat its food, preferring to stand and snip off the bamboo leaves with its teeth. Both red and giant pandas have been hunted for their pelts but, as with many other species, it is human population expansion that is now much more to blame for their status as an endangered species.

It is the lowland's rich red soil that has conferred the name of 'Red Basin' on this area of Sichuan. At one time the Red Basin

Above: The red panda's masked face gives a clue to its link with the racoon family

Opposite: Temminck's Tragopan (Tragopan temmincki), another rare denizen of Sichuan's mountain forests

was covered with broadleaf evergreen forest, but now, shorn of its woodland for more than 2000 years, it is China's most productive agricultural area. Here, crops of tea, maize, sweet potatoes, tobacco, rice and sugar-cane are grown, the moderate climate and rich soil supporting up to three harvests in a single year. Many of the hills are terraced and the structured luxuriance of these low-walled fields, some clinging to 45 degree slopes, is a distinctive feature of the Red Basin.

China's lowland species, such as the tiger and the leopard, have suffered a severe decline in numbers or have become extinct because of agriculture and disturbance in the valleys. In Sichuan the low-lying area is vast – 500 000 km² (193 000 square miles) of habitable land the size of France – but it is still not big enough for the population of 100 million people who, year by year, inch their way further up the mountainside.

For more than three millennia, the same fields have produced crop after crop and, according to Chinese beliefs, the soil owed this impressive fecundity to the mountains, the source of life-giving rain. Hidden by cloud and sheltering the sources of springs, the mountains were believed to create the moisture on which the fruitfulness of the lowland harvest depended, and with it, the whole edifice of civilised life. Small wonder, then, that throughout the length and breadth of the Middle Kingdom, the high peaks were sacred. In panda habitat alone there are as many as a dozen sacred mountains. Song dynasty landscapes juxtaposed the insignificance of humanity with the might of Nature by depicting Man and his works as minuscule against the towering peaks. The very mass of these mountains stabilised the surrounding land and guaranteed the regularity of the seasons. The Chinese built temples to communicate with the spirits of the mountains, and through paintings, sculpture and the arts, glorified the sacred peaks and the animals and plants that lived there.

The mountains of Sichuan, Gansu and Shaanxi are Nature's multi-storey hotels. They are divided into a number of vertical bands, or 'floors', of vegetation, different plants and animals being confined to specific altitudinal zones. These zones are primarily dependent on temperature, which decreases by 1°C for every 100 m (330 ft) or so increase in altitude. Similar 'floors' are found a few storeys higher up a mountain the further south one goes. In general, the bands follow a definite zonal pattern, from lowland evergreen forest, through mixed broadleaf and conifer woodland, to forests consisting almost totally of firs. Above these floors are alpine meadows. The highest peaks are those with a penthouse suite of permanent snow.

The alpine meadow ecosystem lies between the snowline and the first trees. It is a harsh land of rock escarpments and scree slopes that is snowbound for more than six months of the year, a landscape that appears lifeless only until spring conjures the delicate blooms of cushion plants from the stony ground. The alpine meadows are sparsely populated with animals by lower floor standards, but one creature that they do sustain is well adapted to the conditions. The Tibetan marmot, a plump sturdy rodent, survives by sleeping through most of the winter months. One Chinese name for marmot translates as 'haystacker', an allusion to the animal's habit of gathering food plants and piling them in heaps to dry in the sun. The small haystacks are eventually carried underground and provide vital nourishment during the cold, hard days of winter. A family group of up to six animals hibernates together in a special hibernation chamber, waking every three or four weeks to defaecate, urinate and feed on their stored food.

Winter can be more of a problem for insects living on these stark peaks. They labour under a double disadvantage when it comes to cold weather; they are cold blooded and quickly take on the temperature of their surroundings; and being so small, their surface to volume ratio is very high and any heat they may have is rapidly lost to the atmosphere. Most insects either migrate or burrow deep beneath the trunks of trees, or underground, to escape the lethal cold. A few produce a special anti-freeze which prevents their tissues from freezing.

Burrowing beneath the soil is another strategy for avoiding the cold. In spring the Chinese 'grass-worm' can be seen as a thin stalk pushing its way out of the earth after a long winter 'hibernation'. Strangely, at the base of the stalk, some 15 cm (6 ins) below ground, is a dead caterpillar. The secret of this odd amalgam is a fungus which infects the caterpillar in spring, producing fungal strands that drive

Above: Alpine meadow plants are quick to exploit landslips, as does bamboo at lower altitudes

Opposite: The Min Shan Mountains, Wanglang Valley. Mixed deciduous and conifer forest with alpine peaks beyond. The 'meadow' in the foreground is the result of clear-felling

deep into the tissues of the unfortunate insect. In the autumn, when the insect burrows beneath the surface to pupate, the fungus attacks in earnest. It kills the hapless caterpillar and puts the insect's tissues to its own use. The following spring, a fungal shoot bursts from the top of the dead caterpillar's head and grows rapidly into the long, characteristic stalk which, once clear of the earth, releases its spores to the wind to begin the cycle anew. The grass-worm is important in Chinese traditional medicine; cooked in chicken stew, it is said to be a great restorative. Wild plants and animals feature prominently in Chinese medicine and many of these, such as the musk deer (whose musk gland is reputed to reduce fevers) and black bear (bear's claw is eaten for muscular strength), are found in the forest zones below the alpine meadow.

The forest begins between 3000 m to 2600 m (10 000 ft to 8500 ft) as a band of firs, *Abies faxoniana*. A few hardy broadleafed species such as birch, *Betula utilis* and *B. albosinensis*, begin to break into the tall, cathedral-like stands of pine even at this height, but for the most part the forest is pure conifer. At this level, high-altitude bamboo, such as *Sinarundinaria* sp., is also in evidence in the understorey, growing strongly in well-established stands. Most clumps establish themselves either during die-back (when the entire population of mature bamboo flower, seed and die en masse) or when a landslip, or other natural disturbance, lets light into the gloomy forest floor, allowing the buried seed the opportunity to germinate. This is true panda habitat, the bamboo forest so talked about by conservationists and scientists. The understorey is dominated by vast swathes of the giant grass and shrubs and herbs are sparse. It is here that the giant panda and red panda live out their secret lives. The red panda's upper altitudinal limit is several hundred metres higher than the giant panda's because it is more agile and can cope with the steeper slopes that giant pandas tend to avoid.

Rhododendron, too, dot the understorey. The mountains of Sichuan boast more than 300 species of rhododendrons, plants now familiar to gardeners throughout the West, but unknown before the nineteenth century, when the first glorious blooms were brought back.

For the Chinese, these plants are rich in myth and symbolism. The rhododendron and cuckoo share the same Chinese pictogram, derived from the name of an ancient king of Sichuan who was brutally ousted from his palace by his brother. Legend has it that when the heartbroken king died he was transformed into a cuckoo and his tears of sorrow fell to the ground and became bright red rhododendrons. But rhododendrons are deadly as well as beautiful. The plants secrete a poison from their leaves which, when washed into the soil by the mountains' copious rainfall, renders the soil around the plants totally sterile, so removing any possibility of botanical competitors. Small wonder that rhododendrons are biologically very successful.

Sichuan's mountains are home to many species of pheasant, each confined to separate levels of the mountain and many choosing mates with a spectacular courtship display. Sichuan is noted as being the ancient dispersal point of the pheasants, the family evolving in this region and spreading out over much of the Old World. Above the timberline, in the alpine meadows and ranging up as far as the permanent snows, the blood pheasant and the rare, spectacularly beautiful Chinese monal reign supreme. Here, within the conifer belt, lives Temminck's tragopan, and at increasingly lower altitudes, the orange-collared koklass, the white-eared pheasant and the golden pheasant.

In the tree canopy that shelters the giant panda and red panda lives one of the most strikingly attractive inhabitants of the conifer forests – the golden monkey, *Rhinopithecus roxellanae*. Their blue faces and snub-noses framed by a thick golden mane make them stand out among the crowd. Golden monkeys eat buds, fruit, tree bark and lichens. Their thick coat is a necessary adaptation to the winter cold of the mountains where the deep blanket of snow remains from October to April. At one time, only mandarins were allowed to use capes made from this species' fur. Golden monkeys range south into Guizhou and tropical Yunnan.

The Tibetan macaque, *Macaca thibetana*, is another primate found throughout the high peaks of western China. The animals move through the mountains in troops of up to 100 in search of young leaves, fruit and, in spring, birds' eggs. Each troop is headed by a big

*Above: Tibetan macaque female grooming a juvenile on the edge of a
300-foot precipice*

*Opposite: Tibetan macaques share the panda's habitat. This female's
red face shows that she is fully mature*

alpha male, who can weigh a massive 17 kg (37 lbs).[1] The alpha male reigns supreme over his females and the rest of the troop until he is ousted by a stronger, younger competitor.[2] These macaques have a reputation for ferocity. Even on Mount Emei Shan, Sichuan's well-known Buddhist mountain, where the macaque troops are at their most tame, the big alpha males are startlingly aggressive towards visitors. On a number of occasions members of a troop have approached visitors, expecting to be fed. If not immediately offered a titbit, a monkey might well rush up and snatch a bag, or worse, swipe at someone's pockets. On one occasion a young woman was accosted by a big male demanding food while she was taking photos in front of Hungchongping temple. The male suddenly lunged for the woman's handbag and drove his canines into her hand. Seconds later, the culprit was seen up a tree ripping the handbag apart and scattering the inedible contents about the forest. Such alpha males get the pick of the offerings. Even when they have filled their bellies to bursting they still continue to take advantage of their status and pack their cheek pouches (the monkey equivalent of a doggy-bag) with food before yielding place to the troop's number two in the hierarchy.

Tibetan macaques extend down through the conifer forest to the next level, between 2600 and 2000 m (8500 and 6500 ft), where broadleaf trees like *Betula*, *Acer*, *Prunus* and *Pterocarya* begin to share the canopy with evergreens such as *Picea* and *Tsuga*. Nowhere is bamboo growth more luxuriant than at these levels, with larger species such as *Fargesia robusta* reaching heights of 2 m (6 ft) or more. *Fargesia* is especially important to giant pandas during the spring.

There are plants growing here that are almost as rare and threatened as the pandas. The dawn redwood or 'dinosaur tree', *Metasequoia glyptostroboides*, was believed to have been extinct for 20 million years, but in 1944 was found thriving in Sichuan. When journalist Milton Silverman visited China in 1948 to see the trees for himself he wrote: 'we found a lost world – a world that existed more than a million years ago.' The Chinese know the dawn redwood as the water larch. It is shaped like a swamp cypress and, like them, thrives in wet conditions. At 42 m (140 ft) in height and 2 m (6 ft) in diameter it is less than half the size of North American redwoods, and is the only redwood that is deciduous. Its tall stately shape is used to decorate towns and it is now grown as a timber crop in several areas of central and south-eastern China. Farmers also once used the leaves and shoots as fodder for their cattle.

Distributed throughout the bamboo forest is another 'living fossil', the gingko. Known also as the maidenhair tree, it has survived almost unchanged for 200 million years. It first became known to botanists in the West in 1690 when Engelbert Kaempfer published his writings of his visit to Japan. In 1730 the first plant arrived in Utrecht and a tree planted in 1754 still stands in Kew Gardens in Richmond, London. In Palaeozoic times, the gingko was distributed throughout the world, including North America, Eurasia, Australia and the Isle of Mull. Mature trees tower 24 m (80 ft) above the bamboo understorey that is panda territory and, depending on local conditions, can be either narrow or broadly spreading. The gingko is a deciduous tree with distant ancestral links to conifers, but its leaves are in no way needle-like nor does it produce cones. Gingko leaves are like long-stemmed fans with scalloped edges and a deep central notch, a shape which prompted one sixteenth-century Chinese writer to call it the 'duck's-foot tree'. Gingko is actually the modern name for the Japanese version of the Chinese 'yin-kuo', meaning silver fruit. The gingko's male and female flowers produce yellow, plum-shaped fruit that give off an offensive smell when crushed but which contain edible seeds. In days past, the gingko was a prominent feature of Chinese and Japanese temple gardens: its beauty inspired the soul of the initiate, and its kernels, when roasted, provided sustenance for his body. Traditionally, a little *maotai*, China's equivalent of whisky, was said to help the appreciation of both the gingko's beauty and its flavour.

The diverse forest habitat of tall trees and bamboo understorey supports a plethora of animals besides the giant panda and red panda. Beneath the shadowed canopy of the bamboo belt browse herds of takin. A type of goat-antelope, the takin has a heavily built body, long backward-sweeping horns and a prominent, humped snout that the nineteenth-century explorer, H S Wallace, described as a 'Roman nose'.

Earthquakes are common in panda country. This takin was crushed to death by an earthquake-induced landslip

Its yellow coat, the legendary golden fleece of Jason and the Argonauts, is well oiled to protect it from the wet, foggy atmosphere. The endangered white-lipped deer also lives in the bamboo zone, sharing its leafy habitat with sambar, two species of muntjak, and musk deer which, despite domestication for the perfume trade, are still trapped in the wild for their glands. Besides the two panda species, the only other animal in the forest that depends exclusively on bamboo is the bamboo rat, *Rhizomys sinense*. The king-sized rodent leads a subterranean life and has an extensive network of tunnels that may cover an area the size of a suburban garden (200 m^2, or 2000 square ft).

With such a wealth of food at hand, the carnivores are well represented: civets, martens, weasels, three species of badger, lynx, clouded leopard and small cats such as the golden cat. The golden cat comes in so many different colours and patterns, from uniform golden-brown to a black-spotted version, that it is easily mistaken for several different species. It can climb well but hunts mainly on the forest floor, rodents, such as the bamboo rat, being its usual prey, but it will sometimes partake of animals as large as muntjaks and hog deer. Leopards are now rare in panda country, but the few that survive pose a real threat to giant panda cubs and sub-adults, and to red pandas of all ages.

Running through all these vegetation zones are the streams and waterfalls that support another wholly separate layer of life. In this watery domain the soothing white noise of stream and cataract harmonises with the calls of 'piano' frogs, whose music has been celebrated in poetry and song in centuries past. Breeding adults excavate burrows by the stream bank in which to lay their eggs, while other species of frog opt for fastening their eggs under waterfalls with the amphibian equivalent of superglue. The tadpole of *Megophrys* spp. has an extendable mouth that is almost as large as its entire body. The mouth is used as a float as well as a funnel for sucking in plankton and other food.

Below 1600 m (5200 ft), the mixed conifer and broadleaf band of forest gives way to evergreen broadleaf forest including poplar, *Cercodiphyllum* and oak. Or rather, such forests did once exist over a wide lowland area. In times past, the pandas' range undoubtedly extended deep into this benign vegetation zone. But today, the lower limit of the giant panda's and red panda's range, and that of the bamboo forest itself, is no longer set by altitude, but by agriculture. Terraces of maize often reach up as far as 2000 m (6500 ft) and almost everything below this contour is under the sway of humans, a landscape of field upon field of crops. Every year the fragile band of panda habitat is eroded, from below by rising terraces, and from within by logging activity. It is this combination of logging and agriculture that is driving the pandas towards extinction, less than 175 years since they were first 'discovered' by the West.

High rainfall gives rise to numerous streams and cataracts; these not
only allow pandas to drink, but are also home to frog and fish species
unique to panda country

CHAPTER 2

DISCOVERY

With a simple, laconic note in his diary, the French missionary and biologist, Père Armand David, introduced the white bear (soon to be known as the giant panda) to Western science:

> 'My Christian hunters returned today after a ten-day absence. They bring me a white bear, which they took alive but unfortunately killed so that it could be carried more easily. The young white bear, which they sell to me very dearly, is all white except for the legs, ears and around the eyes, which are deep black. The colours are the same as those I saw in the skin of an adult bear the other day at the home of Li, the hunter. This must be a new species of "Ursus", very remarkable not only because of its colour, but also for its paws which are hairy underneath, and for other characteristics.'[3]

The date was 23 March 1869, a day of triumph for Père Armand, who had struggled against almost insurmountable difficulties in his quest for the mysterious *Bai Xiong* of Sichuan.

Though new to Europeans, the Chinese had known of the white bear's existence for over 2000 years. The Empress Dowager Bo was buried in the Nangling Mausoleum near the then capital city of Xian some time between 179–163 BC. When her tomb was opened more than 2100 years later, it was found that the skull of a giant panda had been buried alongside her.[4] The Western Han dynasty (206 BC – AD 24) author Simao Xiangru records that in Xian, the emperor had a garden containing forty of the rarest animals in the known world. The most valued of all was the giant panda. This association of giant panda with Xian is not entirely unexpected. The former capital lies only 120 km (75 miles) to the north-east of Foping, in the Qin Ling Mountains where, to this day, the white bear can still be found. During the fifth century, the first emperor of the Tang dynasty bestowed the pelts of fourteen giant pandas upon an equal number of honoured guests during one of the lavish imperial banquets. This same emperor's grandson is thought to have sent two living pandas, along with an undisclosed number of pelts, to Japan to help cement trade relations between the two countries.[5] With their thick, dense fur giant panda pelts were the ancient Chinese equivalent of the duvet. They were also credited, less plausibly, with protecting a sleeper from ghostly visitations.

Exactly when the name giant panda is first mentioned in Chinese literature is still hotly debated in academic circles; the Chinese used several different names for what appears to be the giant panda. Sadly, the same names are used to describe creatures which are quite obviously not panda. In the *Ben Cao Gang Mu*, a treatise on medicine published in 1578, Li Shizhen quoted from a book of the earlier Eastern Han dynasty (AD 25–220) in which a creature called the *mo* is described as looking: 'like a bear, has a yellowish colour and lives in Sichuan. The annals of the county of Nan Zhong note that it is the size of a donkey, has a whitish colour and resembles a bear … its pelt is good for keeping warm'.

This passage seems to make it obvious that the *mo* and the giant panda are one and the same. Unfortunately, in a poem by the famous Tang dynasty (AD 618–907) poet Bo Juyi, we read that the *mo*: 'has the nose of an elephant, eyes of a rhinoceros, tail of an ox and feet of a tiger. It lives in the valleys of the south'. This description more readily suggests a tapir, apart from the tiger's feet, than a giant panda.

An ancient name for what seems to be the giant panda was *pi*

Tales of a mysterious 'white bear' inspired Père Armand David in his search for Sichuan's unknown species

or *pixiu*. The first mention of the animal was probably in the *Book of History*, written over 3000 years ago during the Western Chou dynasty (1066–71 BC). Here the phrase 'like a tiger and a pi' appears. The *Book of Songs*, the earliest known collection of Chinese poetry, contains the line: 'to present the pelt of a pi'. And just to confuse matters, the earliest known dictionary from China, the *Er Ya* (Qin dynasty, 221–207 BC), defines a pi as a white fox. This same book goes on to describe the *mo* as a white leopard with a small head, short limbs, and black and white markings, a description that must refer to the giant panda.

Whatever name they chose to describe the giant panda, one habit which many of the ancient texts describe sounds very strange to the modern reader – the beast is said to eat metal, usually copper and iron. *The Classics of Seas and Mountains* (770–256 BC) gives an accurate description of a 'bearlike, black and white animal that … lives in the Qionglai Mountains south of Yandao County', but then goes on to say that it 'eats copper and iron'. The *Ben Cao Gang Mu*, quoted above, also states that 'the animal licks iron and may eat 10 jin [approximately 5 kg, or 11 lbs] at a time'. *Er Ya* gets it right, and wrong, by stating that the *mo* licks and eats bamboo stems, iron and copper.

George Schaller[6] believes that the metal-eating story probably derives from the giant panda's habit of visiting homesteads for food, licking out cooking pots, and sometimes even chewing up the stewpots and saucepans with its strong teeth, in an effort to get the food remnants. This explanation is almost certainly correct. In Wolong Giant Panda Reserve we spoke to several researchers who had spent weeks working high in the mountains at the Wuyipeng Research Station. They told us of waking in the morning to find crumpled pots and pans lying outside their tents, the result of a night-time incursion by hungry pandas.

It was stories of this strange, iron-eating beast that spurred on Père Armand David in his search for the white bear. A Basque by birth, as a boy he thought nothing of walking ten or twelve hours a day, collecting butterflies, observing insects and watching the behaviour of birds and mammals. Very early in his life, Armand David decided what course his life should take. Much to the chagrin of his father, a respected doctor who had hoped his son would follow in his footsteps, the young Armand announced that he would join the priesthood and become a missionary. This latter ambition took a great deal of time and effort. A letter he wrote to Bishop Mouly in 1852 describes the depth of this commitment:

> 'The more my natural tastes are satisfied the more I am strengthened in my first resolve. I fear I might lose the vocation for which I was confirmed and in which I was encouraged by my director, Fr Martin; indeed, for the past twelve years I am pursued with the thought of dying while working at the saving of unbelievers. It is this desire which caused me to become a priest and to come to the mission [at Savona in Italy, where he was employed, unhappily, as a teacher of science]. I am getting on in years and am almost twenty-seven, and want to go to the Celestial Empire, Mongolia, and other similar places as soon as possible in order to learn new languages, customs and climates. Thank God my health is excellent and my always robust constitution will enable me to undergo the life, fatigue and privations of a missionary. However, I cannot say the same of other qualities I wish I had. Alas! My desire to go to the missions is motivated in part by a desire to do penance, but also by the belief that since childhood God has called me to this.'[7]

It took much wheedling and cajoling but eventually Armand (now Père Armand) got his wish. After almost a decade of pleading his case he was finally sent to China as a missionary, rejoicing in the knowledge that he could now begin the work of saving souls. But the Fates and his own natural inclinations led him along a different path. Just before leaving for Beijing (known in those days as Peking), his spiritual fathers introduced him to the Director of the Museum of Natural History in Paris, Henri Milne-Edwards. Milne-Edwards was desperate to catalogue any and all specimens that might be collected in China. Knowing of the young priest's interest in biology, he asked Père Armand if he would keep his eye open for any unusual specimens that could be caught and shipped back to Paris. Père Armand agreed. It was to be a fateful decision.

Soon after arriving in Beijing, Armand heard rumours of a strange beast, known to the Chinese as *ssu-pu-hsiang*, 'the four aspects which do not match', a creature said to possess the tail of a donkey, hooves of a cow, neck of a camel and the antlers of a stag. As with all other important treasures in China, this fabled beast was owned by the emperor, and said to reside in the Nan Haizi hunting park to the south of Beijing, one of the many imperial gardens and parks near the capital which allowed the emperor to escape the closeted, claustrophobic atmosphere of the Forbidden City. The park was enclosed by a high wall, over 70 km (43 miles) in circumference and guarded by Tartar soldiers, who, being far from home, were thought to be less likely to disobey the imperial edict against visitors. Entrance to the park was forbidden to all, Chinese and foreigners alike, on pain of death. For a *yang guezi* (foreign devil) to be found in its environs was to invite arrest, or worse.

Père David ignored the dangers. Unable to contain his curiosity, in September 1865 he visited Nan Haizi hunting park in secret, scouting stealthily around the perimeter in the hope of finding a position from which to view the park's forbidden secrets. It was a risky strategy, but it succeeded; after several miles Père David found that a portion of the wall was undergoing repairs. It was late in the day, and the builders had already left their work. By standing on a pile of bricks he was able to bring his head above the level of the wall. What he saw startled and excited him. The *ssu-pu-hsiang* were no fable. They were deer, but unlike any deer Père David had seen before. Standing around 120 cm (47 ins) tall at the shoulder, and covered in a pelt of grey-brown fur, the strange deer did indeed accord with their Chinese name, a hotch-potch of features drawn from several other animals. Their tails were longer than those of any known deer and ended in a dark 'brush', more like a donkey than a deer. Their gait, too, resembled a member of the horse, not the deer, tribe. Their feet were remarkable; the cloven hooves bending upwards like a sultan's shoes. Even their antlers were unusual; they seemed to have been taken from another deer species, turned back to front and stuck onto the unfortunate *ssu-pu-hsiang*'s head.

To Père David, the sight of such a beast at close hand was absolutely irresistible. At great personal risk, he contrived to bribe one of the Tartar guards to obtain the bones and pelt of one of these splendid deer. The price was copper cash worth 20 taels. Had they have been caught in their transaction, the price would have been higher – the penalty for killing a *ssu-pu-hsiang* was death. The illicit remains were sent via an attaché at the French Legation, Alphonse Pichon, to Henri Milne-Edwards in Paris. The specimen created an unprecedented interest. Père David's reputation as a collector was greatly enhanced and he was asked by no lesser personage than the Minister of Public Instruction to ship live specimens of this unique creature back to France. A herd of these animals (now called *Elaphurus davidianus*, Père David's deer) still live at Nan Haizi Park.

Over the following years David and several others managed to send a number of *ssu-pu-hsiang* back to Europe. Many of these specimens died, but a group of four sent in 1870 (two from Père David and a further two from the French Embassy) began breeding. This was far more fortunate than anyone could have imagined at that time. Unknown to any Westerner, the animals confined in the imperial hunting park at Nan Haizi were the last of their race; the species had been wiped out in the wild many years before. When, in 1894, the Han River overflowed its banks and broke through the walls of the *ssu-pu-hsiang*'s last sanctuary, most of the herd were slaughtered by peasants who had been left destitute by the floods. The few that remained were shot during the Boxer Rebellion by Western troops. Happily, the few Père David's deer in the West continued to thrive and breed. In 1896 two deer, offspring of the original four that had been shipped to Paris in 1870, were set free at Woburn Abbey, the Duke of Bedford's estate in Bedfordshire. Just over sixty years later, four descendants of these two deer were returned to Beijing for breeding. The Marquess of Tavistock, in collaboration with the World Wildlife Fund, sent a further nineteen deer to China in November 1985. There is no doubt that had it not been for the intrepid French priest, 'the four aspects which do not match' would not have survived into the twentieth century.

Even before his attempts to find the white bear, Père David had discovered a prodigious number of new Chinese species. He introduced numerous plants to Western science, and to Western gardens, many of which still bear his name: *Buddleia davidii, Lilium davidii, Adonis davidii, Clematis armandii, Clematis davidiana, Viburnum davidii, Prunus davidiana, Stranvaesia davidiana*; the list is endless. Perhaps the most important find, among the flowers, was *Davidia involucrata*, the dove tree of Sichuan which owes its name to the pair of enormous white bracts that surround each blossom in spring, making the tree look as if it is covered by a flock of white doves. He discovered almost 100 new species of insect, including butterflies such as the gloriously coloured *Armandia thaitina, Lycaena atroguttata, Lycaxna coeligena* and *Pieris davidis*. Birds figured greatly in his collection (he discovered 58 species in all) including the pheasant, *Crossoptilon auritum*, the passerines *Pyrgilauda davidi* and *Propasser davidianus*, and an owl, *Syrnium davidi*. Hunters brought some specimens to him (and were paid handsomely for their efforts) but the missionary was also a good shot himself.

Although always ready to use his rifle in the service of science, Père David refused to hunt for the pot:

> 'I observe the principle of never killing an animal not needed for my natural history collections I find it less distressing to feed myself with only rice or millet than to kill one of these poor creatures, who revel in life so joyously and do not harm nature, but on the contrary embellish it. This attitude is not always agreeable to my servants, especially when it is a question of pheasants, but I hold firmly to my rule.'

Fish were caught by a variety of methods, not all of them orthodox. On one occasion, at Jiujiang, a town close to both the Yangtze River and the famous lake, the Poyang Hu, the townsfolk held a ceremony to appease the wrath of the local water gods. Part of the ritual called for paper lanterns of every size, colour and shape to be placed on the water. The oil that fuelled the lanterns came from the nut of the plant, *Aleurites fordii*, which proved lethal to fish whenever it leaked into the water. Many of these fish found their way into the collection of the opportunistic Père Armand. Unfortunately, another Chinese product proved less helpful. Armand stored the fish in Chinese alcohol, believing it to be as effective as Western alcohol for preservation of specimens. A few weeks later his precious specimens had turned into a thick fish soup.

Despite all these finds it is with his mammalian discoveries that Père Armand's name is associated. Apart from the Père David's deer, he was responsible for introducing numerous new species of mammal to the West. Some were collected on his first expedition to Mongolia, such as the red-brown squirrel, *Sciurus davidianus*, and the jerboa, *Dipus annulatus*, a tiny sand-coloured rodent similar in appearance to a kangaroo with enormous hind feet, large ears and a long thin tail which ended in a wide, black and white 'brush'. *Siphneus armandii*, a golden-furred rodent, was also discovered during the expedition, which lasted a little over eight months, from 12 March to 26 October 1866.

Two further collecting trips followed the Mongolian expedition, the first a two-year journey to central China and eastern Tibet, the second a north-south journey of some twenty months, from Beijing to the southern provinces of Jiangxi and Fujian. But it was the journey to central China, and especially the time Père Armand spent among the foothills of the Tibetan Plateau, that ensured that the name of the indomitable Frenchman earned a place in history.

The historic journey began, in May 1868. Travelling from Beijing to Shanghai by sea, Père David undertook the arduous journey up the Yangtze River, a waterway that was navigable in its upper reaches only by man-hauling and poling through dangerous, often fatal, rapids. The incessant turmoil of the journey began to tell on Père David, as he recorded in his diary of 16 December: 'I begin to feel very tired, morally and physically, and it seems as if this tyrannical navigation will never end'. After innumerable adventures, including losing their boat and being almost run down by another runaway vessel, they reached Chengdu in January 1869.

Less than two weeks later, on 15 January, Père David, together with Ouang-Thomé, a Chinese Christian convert, and four porters, set off across the featureless landscape of Sichuan's Red Basin. His aim

The forests of Sichuan are home to the greatest profusion of plant and animal species anywhere in the temperate latitudes

was to stay at a small Christian college in the village of Ho-pa-ch'ang where he could acclimatise himself to conditions in the forbidding western mountains. His ultimate goal was the fabled principality of Muping, set on the rim of the eastern Tibetan highlands, where he hoped to find the legendary white bear, and much else besides. He was not overly optimistic, referring to Muping ironically as: 'the promised land, where everyone says there are marvels', adding, 'I admit, however, that I am not over-enthusiastic, remembering the number of times I have been misled by Chinese promises'.

Père David spent a month on this reconnaissance. He stayed at the house of a celebrated hunter, a Mr Ho, who had converted to Christianity some years before. The region was plagued with brigands, and during his stay a nearby house was plundered. Mr Ho set off in pursuit with fifty villagers, caught the bandits dividing the spoils, and executed them. Such occurrences were by no means uncommon; brigands were a fact of life in this part of China. Père David accepted the risks with characteristic stoicism:

'If I am to be held back by fears of this kind I shall never do any exploring since the wild places, reputed to be the haunts of thieves and murderers, are precisely the ones that offer the most in the way of natural history in China. For safety only and to assuage evil intentions I shall make sure to keep my gun much in evidence.'

Père David returned with his own priceless plunder from this exploration. He discovered the takin (*Budorcas taxicolor*), a goat-antelope with odd lyre-shaped horns and a coat that can range in colour from reddish-brown to a startling gold. Some authorities believe that the Greek myth of Jason and the golden fleece refers to a takin skin that had somehow found its way to Colchis. He had also collected over fifty-five specimens of birds, some of them previously unknown.

The celebrations of the Chinese New Year intervened after his return to Chengdu, but on 22 February 1869 the intrepid Frenchman was ready to begin the journey to his 'promised land'. Once again, he was accompanied by Ouang-Thomé. Four porters carried his meagre personal baggage and his scientific equipment. By 1 March they were in Muping, at a Christian college that had been founded fifty years earlier, during one of the periodic persecutions of Christians that had forced the missionaries to flee to this remote spot. Père David made the college his base-camp from which to mount sorties into the surrounding mountains in search of the white bear and other wonders. Ten days later a chance meeting gave Père David his first evidence that the white bear was reality and not myth. As David and his hunters rested on the remains of some felled pines, a prosperous-looking man appeared on the path. This was Mr Li, the largest landowner in the area. He invited the party to his house for tea and sweets. What Père David saw there, affixed to a wall of the landowner's sitting room, must have set his heart beating wildly:

'I see at this pagan's house a skin of the famous black and white bear, which appears to be very large. It is a remarkable species, and I am overjoyed when my hunters tell me that I will certainly procure this animal in a little while; tomorrow, they tell me, they will go out and kill this carnivore which should make an interesting novelty for science.'

The hunters were as good as their word; it took a further twelve days, but on 23 March Père David took possession of the body of a freshly killed, young white bear. One week after they brought in a second animal, also dead, this time an adult female:

'Its colours are exactly like those of the young one I have, only the darker parts are less black and the white more soiled. [Wild pandas are rarely the well-scrubbed, pristine black and white animals seen in zoos.] The animal's head is very big, and the snout round and short instead of being pointed as it is in the Asian black bear.'

Père David was the first to recognise the significance of this new beast. Given his location, deep in central China, he would not be able to show the pelt or other artefacts for some considerable time. As a compromise, he sent word of his find by courier to Professor Alphonse Milne-Edwards, son of the Director of the Paris Museum of Natural History, describing it as: '… a bear which seems to me to be new to science', and continuing with a detailed description:

'*Ursus melanoleucus*, A.D. (Armand David, not Anno Domini!). Very large according to my hunters. Ears short. Tail very short. Hair fairly short; beneath the four feet very hairy. Colours: white, with the ears, the surrounding of the eyes, the tip of the tail and the four legs brownish black. The black on the forelegs is joined over the back in a straight band. I have just received a young bear of this kind and I have seen the mutilated skins of adult specimens. The colours are always the same and equally distributed. I have not seen this species, which is easily the prettiest kind of animal I know, in the museums of Europe. Is it possible that it is new to science?'

Muping was indeed a land of wonders. On 4 May his hunters brought Père David yet more marvels, six monkeys of an altogether unknown species which the Chinese called *Chin-tsin-hou*. They were massive primates, their shoulders covered in a magnificent cape of golden fur. But it was their faces that most surprised Père David: a tiny, upturned nose sat in the middle of a face that was covered in the most startling blue skin. The species is known today as the golden monkey, *Rhinopithecus roxellanae*. The species' name honours Roxellana, a Galician girl of unsurpassed beauty who was abducted by Turkish raiders and eventually found her way into the harem of Sultan Suleiman the Magnificent. Her tiny nose, immense blue eyes and hair of russet gold so charmed the sultan that in 1523 he took 'the favoured shining one' as his wife, the first sultan in more than 400 years to marry. When the specimens of the *Chin-tsin-hou* arrived in Paris, Alphonse Milne-Edwards was so struck by the tilted nose and golden cape of hair that he named the startlingly beautiful primate after the equally stunning slave-girl. What would the original Roxellana have made of the monkey's blue face?

Between the discovery of the white bear and the golden monkey

Père David's hunters also brought him a firefox, a beautiful beast with glowing, almost incandescent russet-red fur, a pointed fox-like face, masked like a racoon, and a long, ringed tail. The beast was already known to Père David as the 'panda'. An extract from his diary reads:

'The panda is an interesting animal already known in the Himalayas and formally abundant in these forests but now scarce. My hunters tell me that this plantigrade animal lives in trees and in holes, and that its food is vegetable or animal according to the occasion. The Chinese call it "child of the mountain" because its voice imitates that of a child.'

The 'panda' had been discovered more than seventy-eight years earlier by a Danish botanist, Nathaniel Wallich. Wallich was director of the East India Company's Botanic Gardens, based in Calcutta, but he was evidently also interested in zoology. As was often the case in the early days of the biological sciences, specialisation in one subject did not preclude interest and expertise in another. Wallich handed the pelt over to another amateur zoologist, a British army officer, Major-General Thomas Hardwicke. The pelt was shown at a meeting of the Linnaean Society in 1821. Unfortunately, neither of these men bothered to publish a formal scientific description of the new species. The scientific laurels were eventually claimed some four years later, in 1825, when the famous zoologist, Frédéric Cuvier, gave details of a second specimen sent to him by his son-in-law, Alfred Du Vaucel. Cuvier proposed the name Ailurus, meaning cat-like, for all members of the genus and the species name *fulgens* 'because of its brilliant colours', which were apparent even after preservation and the long sea journey to France.

Père David was an astute enough zoologist to recognise that there were similarities between the 'child of the mountain' and the new species he believed he had discovered. Writing of the panda, he notes: 'Its paws and head resemble those of my white bear'. But, lacking the equipment to perform a full anatomical description of the beast, he very sensibly assumed that the creature he had discovered was a bear, hence the appellation *Ursus melanoleucus*.

It was only in Paris that problems began to arise. Alphonse Milne-Edwards was the first to dissect the beast and he discovered a number of anatomical features that made him doubt that the white bear should be assigned to the *Ursidae* (the bears). In particular, its skeletal and especially its dental characteristics more closely resembled those of the racoons and the panda of the Himalayas, Père David's 'child of the mountain'. He therefore created for the white bear a new genus, which he called *Ailuropoda*, the full species name being *Ailuropoda melanoleuca*, the panda-footed, black and white creature. Père David, at least at the beginning, disagreed with the designation. He tended to believe that the white bear was just that, a bear. So began a dispute that has continued to the present day (see Appendix 2) – is the giant panda an aberrant of the bear, or an oversized racoon?

Whatever its evolutionary background, once the giant panda had been discovered, all the world's museums began clamouring for specimens to display. The task was not an easy one. China was still the 'forbidden kingdom', and while foreigners might be gradually extending their trading concessions and influence on China's coastal regions, inland the 'foreign devil' was still an object of contempt and not a little fear. During the next sixty years or so the only specimens of giant panda obtained by Western zoos came from Chinese hunters by way of missionaries and diplomats, whose gunboats and armed presence could 'persuade' the Chinese government to issue the necessary exit permits.

Hunters, too, found the animal irresistible, and to be the first to effect personally the demise of this beautiful creature became something of a holy grail among the 'big game' fraternity. It is hard to imagine why the killing of this amiable and harmless creature should have so stimulated the desires of the chase. The gorilla, another of Nature's pacifists, was imbued with the characteristics of a demon to justify its destruction. According to contemporary legends, gorillas were monsters, hairy giants who tore hapless natives limb from limb, wreaking mayhem wherever they went unless stopped by the fearless *bwana.* The hunters who went to face the beast thought of themselves as latter-day knights doing battle with the forest ogre.

The giant panda was never regarded as fearsome. Somehow, it was simply accepted that shooting a panda was 'the thing to do'. Perhaps it was the lure of forbidden fruit that attracted hunters. Authority to travel in panda country was rarely given, and the granting of permission to shoot pandas was almost unheard of. It was not until 1928 that a serious attempt at shooting giant panda began. In November of that year two brothers, Kermit and Theodore Roosevelt, left New York for Burma, en route to China. That their request to the Chinese government to kill a giant panda had been granted was due in no small part to the fact that their father happened to be President of the United States. The trip was funded by William V Kelly, a patron of the Field Museum of Chicago, which hoped to display the dead panda should the expedition prove successful.

A little more than three months after their arrival in Rangoon they were in Père Armand's 'promised land', Muping. After almost a week of fruitless searching they moved on. By 23 April they were stalking takin in misty drizzle near Yehli, south-west of Chengdu, when they unexpectedly happened on fresh panda spoor in the snow. They followed it. Hearing a noise, their guide moved off the track, then gestured insistently. Kermit Roosevelt moved to his side as the guide:

> 'pointed to a giant spruce tree thirty yards away. The bole was hollowed, and from it emerged the head and forequarters of a beishung [*bai xiong* – white bear]. He looked sleepily from side to side as he sauntered forth. He seemed very large, and like the animal of a dream.'

For the giant panda it was a nightmare. The two brothers fired simultaneously, killing the animal outright. They were the first Westerners to shoot a giant panda. But not the last. With those two shots the floodgates were opened, and permissions for panda 'collecting expeditions' were granted to several hunters. Not all were successful. Just three more pandas were shot by Westerners, the last by an Englishman, Captain Courtney Brocklehurst. That is not to say that only four giant panda carcasses were exported to the West during this period. Far from it. Between 1928 and 1949, more than a dozen giant panda bodies found their way to European and North American museums. That most of them had been killed by Chinese, not Western, hunters was irrelevant in the face of the damage that such 'collecting' did to the viability of the few pandas remaining in the wild.

Panda shooting as a sport stopped in the mid-thirties, but the attrition on the wild population did not. It intensified, and for one simple reason. Westerners no longer wished to see dead pandas in museum dioramas, they now wanted the real thing – live pandas in their zoos, pandas they could see, hear, touch and smell.

William H Harkness Junior was determined to be the first to give the public what they wanted. A Harvard graduate with a sizeable fortune, Harkness had never set foot in China before his expedition to the Middle Kingdom early in 1935. He left behind him a wife of a few weeks, Ruth Harkness, who, unknown to herself or her husband, was to figure greatly in the story. Harkness's expedition was ill-starred from the outset. The permits necessary to catch a panda proved to be quite as elusive as the panda itself. Harkness spent months jumping through innumerable bureaucratic hoops, but despite all the influence he could bring to bear on the Chinese authorities, the Nanking Academia Sinica finally refused to grant him the necessary permissions.

Harkness's response to this disappointment was to go to ground. While still in Shanghai he simply slipped out of sight, moving to different accommodation and using an assumed name. It may be that he was simply trying to get over his disappointment by cutting himself off from the world he knew. Indeed, that is the explanation he himself offered for his extraordinary behaviour. But it is equally likely that, having been thwarted in his formal attempts to obtain permission, he wished to remain incognito so as to achieve his ends in a less official manner. Whatever the reason, his cover was soon blown and he was hauled before the United States judiciary in Shanghai to account for his actions.

Red pandas are mainly crepuscular; they are most active at dawn and dusk

Harkness then fell in with one Floyd 'Tangier' Smith, a North American professional hunter who had spent much time 'up country' in China collecting for American museums, and Gerald Russel, a young Englishman of independent means who was travelling in China in search of excitement. The three travelled to Sichuan, and were preparing to move into the mountains, presumably with the intention of capturing a giant panda, when a cable from the United States Consul in Hankow ordered them back to eastern China. Depressed and dejected, the two Americans obeyed the summons, leaving Gerald Russel in Sichuan, possibly to prepare for Harkness's third attempt to catch his elusive prey.

It was not to be. William Harkness never again saw Sichuan, or his native land. By February 1936 he was dead; the cause of his death was never officially confirmed.

If Harkness's death was a bolt from the blue, his wife's action following his demise was totally unexpected. On the surface at least, Ruth Harkness was a city-loving sophisticate who was not the least bit interested in zoology. The death of her husband turned her, virtually overnight, into a woman with a mission. She was determined to achieve the ambition her husband had died for and she went about it with iron-willed determination. She needed every ounce of her courage for she was met at every turn by patronising comments and well-meaning advice that she should give up her impossible, self-imposed task. She ignored all comments and ploughed ahead, acknowledging her ignorance of taxonomy, but confident (quite rightly) that the panda was probably the easiest of all beasts to identify. As she herself said: 'certainly it never could be confused with any other animal in the world. The markings are unmistakable.'

Ruth Harkness landed in Shanghai less than a year after her husband had died and immediately set about the task of organising the permissions and logistical support necessary for an expedition into the wilds of Sichuan. The adventures she underwent and the characters she met in her search were the stuff of high adventure and her book *The Lady and the Panda* deservedly became a best seller, especially as, unlike all the men who had tried before her, Ruth Harkness succeeded.

Despite her iron determination, it has to be admitted that luck played a very great part in Ruth Harkness's success. Or perhaps fortune really does favour the brave. After a tiring trip from Shanghai to Chengdu, the expedition moved into the Qionglai Mountains of Sichuan, into the very area that is now the premier giant panda reserve, Wolong. They set up base-camp near Tsaopo village and organised a series of bivouacs in and around the nearby mountain from which they planned to trap the giant panda. After a few days in base-camp, Ruth Harkness was invited by her camp overseer, Quentin Young, to visit one of the trapping bivouacs. No sooner had she arrived (she had visited only a single panda trap), than she heard a gun-shot and much unintelligible shouting in Chinese. Along with Quentin Young, she ran towards the sound. Then Quentin stopped suddenly:

'He listened intently for a split second, and then went ploughing on so rapidly I couldn't keep up with him. Dimly through the waving wet branches I saw him near a huge rotting tree. I stumbled on blindly, brushing the water from my face and eyes. Then I too stopped, frozen in my tracks. From the dead old tree came a baby's whimper.

I must have been momentarily paralysed for I didn't move until Quentin came towards me and held out his arms. There in the palms of his two hands was a squirming baby Bei shung.'[8]

It is hard to escape the feeling that, had one of the many men seeking the giant panda been fortunate enough to find the baby, then it would not have survived the arduous journey back to the United States. Urban sophisticate she might have been, but Ruth Harkness instinctively understood an infant's needs. She had brought with her a baby's nursing bottle and a plentiful supply of dried milk. Harkness and the baby panda, named Su Lin, arrived back in the United States to a blaze of publicity.

It was at this point that the world's love affair with the giant panda really began. It was one thing to see a stuffed panda and marvel at the beauty of its black and white coat. It was quite another to watch

Su Lin's activities in the flesh. This piebald teddy bear's harmless demeanour, bumbling gait and human-like feeding habits were so engaging that the giant panda could not fail to capture the imagination, and the heart, of the world.

But it was very much a one-sided love affair. The giant panda became the zoo equivalent of a Rolls-Royce. Zoo directors in different countries vied with each other to be the first with a live panda on display and the trapping of live pandas continued apace. Some voices were raised in protest. Writing to *The Times* on 17 June 1939, Courtney Brocklehurst drew attention to an article by the editor of *The China Journal* in which the capturing of live pandas was said to be:

'... already seriously threatening the species with extermination. Already, according to Mrs Harkness, who was in that area last spring, two big valleys in the Wassu country, which formerly contained many pandas, have been completely denuded of these animals ... A rare and not too plentiful animal at best the giant panda cannot long survive such persecution ...'

But few took heed of this warning, preferring to ignore the disastrous effect such attrition might have on the wild panda population. Despite an order protecting pandas from capture, issued by the Sichuan provincial government in 1939, it was not until 1946 that the flow of pandas to the West stopped. In that year, under the headline 'Panda on the Brink of Extinction', the Chinese newspaper *Da Gong Bao* sounded the alarm once more, declaring that:

'Pandas living in the border areas of Sichuan and Xikang are becoming very scarce due to intensive capturing at present. Hunters have raised the price of the animal and every couple of months a panda is caught. If the situation goes on like this, the giant panda is likely to become extinct.'

Between 1937 and 1949, when the People's Republic of China was established and the country effectively closed its borders to foreigners, no fewer than fourteen giant panda were exported to foreign zoos. And this takes no account of the terrible toll that export exacted on captive pandas. For every panda that successfully made the transition from mountain to menagerie, several more died while awaiting transhipment because of disease, incorrect feeding or general maltreatment.

Whatever the human cost of China's self-imposed isolation of the fifties and sixties, there is no doubt that the closing of China's borders did much to save the creature from extinction until the more enlightened and ecologically orientated seventies (though it should be noted that the Chinese government had banned hunting and urged protection of the giant panda as early as 1962). This action was timely indeed. Had zoo collection continued at former levels, it is likely that the chances of giant panda survival (slim even today) would now be non-existent.

CHAPTER 3

BAMBOO

No account of pandas in the wild would be meaningful without first looking at its staple food – the bamboo. The behaviour of both species of panda is so intimately meshed with the bamboo's growth and distribution that it would be impossible to understand panda behaviour without reference to the plant.

Bamboo is the king of grasses, a giant that, in terms of height or girth, far surpasses any other member of this ubiquitous family of plants. Although the taxonomy of the bamboo group is still not completely known, the world has upwards of fifty different genera of bamboo, containing in all some 1000 species. The adaptability of the group is astounding. Every continent except Europe and Antarctica can boast native bamboo species, though the group reaches its most extreme forms in South-East Asia. Bamboo can be found from sea-level to mountain slopes at an altitude of over 4000 m (13 000 ft). They range in size from normal grasses through scrambling climbers to goliaths like the tropical *Dendrocalamus giganteus*, 40 m (130 ft) tall and more than 1 m (3 ft) in circumference.

China probably has the largest number of bamboo species of any nation – 300 species comprising twenty-six genera. The Chinese have always prized the bamboo. It is the chief member of the triad known as 'the winter friends', bamboo, pine and plum. For thousands of years, these three plants have symbolised perseverance and resistance against overwhelming odds. The pine thrives and grows tall in poor soil, the plum's blossom opens while the winter snow still lies on the ground, and the evergreen bamboo seems contemptuous of the vicissitudes of the season, bending beneath the weight of snow, but shooting upright again at the first hint of spring.

The Chinese have used the bamboo for centuries to provide for almost all their needs. It has been the means of survival and of destruction, providing tools to plough and work the land and weapons with which to wage war. Bamboo paper has afforded a record of the nation's history unsurpassed anywhere in the world. The first records were inscribed on the protective sheaths of bamboo shoots. These sheaths became the first 'paper' pages; strung together they made the first book. The brush and stylus that recorded these events were in all probability also made of bamboo. Before the introduction of air conditioning and electric fans, many men took solace in a 'bamboo wife', a long cylinder of bamboo basketwork which lay beside the sleeper and allowed cool breezes to pass unhindered. The Chinese transported goods around the country in bamboo bullock-carts and one-wheeled hand-carts that permitted easy access across the narrow, 30 cm (12 ins) wide paths between rice-paddies. People were also transported by bamboo, in litters and palanquins carried by two or four porters. Indeed, in certain inaccessible areas, they still are. On the sacred mountain of Emei Shan, '*hua-ga*', two-man litters made of bamboo, are used to transport pilgrims and tourists up and down the precipitous trails. Film-makers, too. Having been forced on one occasion to use a *hua-ga* to move quickly about the mountains, we can vouch for the efficiency, if not the comfort, of this mode of travel. In crossing rivers, those great barriers to trade and movement, the Chinese also made use of bamboo. On the Min River in Sichuan, there is a bridge constructed almost entirely of bamboo. Great cables of twisted bamboo, almost 20 cm (8 ins) in diameter, support the bridge, which is still in use after more than 1000 years.

Bamboo is also important in Chinese medicine. The underground root of the black bamboo (*Phyllostachys nigra*) is used in the treatment of kidney problems. When heated, the sap that exudes from

*Giant pandas actively seek out
the shoots of umbrella bamboo
during springtime*

the fresh stems of this same species is used, instead of aspirin, to reduce fevers. Another species, *Sinocalamus affinis*, is burned and the ash used to treat prickly heat. Given its shape and rapid growth it would be surprising if the bamboo had escaped an association with the erotic arts. In the south of China, and also in India, a hard amber-like secretion, *tabasheer*, that forms between the nodes of certain species has the reputation for being a sovereign cure for impotence. It can also cure asthma.

Even in this age of plastics, the bamboo is still invaluable to the Chinese. In a street in Chengdu, we saw children playing with bamboo toys, shaded from the hot sun under bamboo awnings, while their younger siblings were wheeled in prams made entirely of bamboo, or rocked to sleep in bamboo cradles by grandparents who sat smoking bamboo pipes in bamboo chairs. Researchers have documented at least 1000 uses for the plant, including roof tiles, musical instruments, gutters and rain-spouts, ladders, irrigation pipes, fencing and rafts. One engineer has even used it to distil a fuel for diesel engines. The usefulness of bamboo seems limited only by the imagination of Man.

But why is it so versatile? The answer lies in its internal structure. The shoots that arise from an underground rhizome grow into woody stems (culms) that are hollow and jointed, conferring both strength and lightness, and making them ideal for many human endeavours. The shoots grow at a truly prodigious rate; no other plant, or animal, grows so tall in so short a period of time. The world record was set in Kyoto, Japan, when a culm of Ma-dake, *Phyllostachys bambusoides*, was recorded as having grown almost 1.3 m (4 ft) in 24 hours, the equivalent of 5 cm (2 ins) an hour. Even at colder, high altitudes the rate of growth is impressive; a shoot of *Fargesia robusta* measured at Wolong Giant Panda Research Station grew a commendable 1 m (3 ft) in five days.

An ancient tradition in China was to visit the bamboo groves at night during early spring and to listen to the popping of the bamboo shoots as they broke explosively from their coverings into the night air. More prosaically, the Chinese regard bamboo shoots as a superior form of food, valuing the crisp texture. Like blanched asparagus, the most succulent bamboo shoots are those that never see the light of day. To achieve this, the peasant farmers walk barefoot through a bamboo grove in early spring, feeling for the tell-tale bumps that signal that a shoot is about to emerge. They cover the spot with a pile of earth, returning a few days later to harvest the crop. A Chinese poet, Bo Juyi, epitomised the Chinese love of bamboo in a ninth-century poem:

'My new province is a land of bamboo groves;
Their shoots in spring fill the valleys and hills.
The mountain woodman cuts an armful of them
And brings them down to sell at the early market
Things are cheap in proportion as they are common;
For two farthings I buy a whole bundle.
I put the shoots in a great earthen pot
And eat them along with boiling rice.
The purple nodules break – like an old brocade,
The white skin opens – like new pearls.'[9]

Many other species are attracted to this seasonal feast of bamboo shoot. Apart from the red and giant pandas, bamboo rat, takin, sambar and tufted deer, wild pig, porcupine and squirrels all take advantage of this nutritional bonanza. Schaller reports that the droppings of one Asiatic black bear (*Ursus [Selenarctos] thibetanus*) in his study area were composed entirely of bamboo shoots. The parrotbill, *Conostoma oemodium*, was also observed visiting the young shoots, using its curved beak to tear away the shoots' protective sheaths and feed on the tender tips. Surprisingly, insects probably take a heavier toll on the emerging shoots than any of these vertebrate predators. Seemingly strong shoots will suddenly stop growing, the tips turning soft, their colour changing from vibrant green to sickly yellow. The cause is insect larvae, particularly of beetles and Anthomiid flies, which live inside the plant, between the nodes, and literally eat it alive. In a three-year period at Wolong, insects killed, on average, 19 per cent of all new shoots produced. Additional research showed that whereas insects chose thin shoots in which to lay their eggs, usually with a diameter of between 0.7–0.9 cm (0.3–0.35 ins), giant pandas selected thicker shoots (see Chapter 4). While this is good for both pandas and insects, as they do not compete with one another for the same resource, it puts the bamboo under twice as much pressure from predators. In the Wolong area insects and pandas together destroy somewhere between 33 per cent and 50 per cent of all new shoots produced every year. Despite its reserve status, much of the remaining wildlife of Wolong has been heavily hunted and is still at low levels. George Schaller and his co-workers believe that where species such as wild pig and bear have not been so heavily culled, the combined grazing pressure on the new shoots could well mean that, in an average year, most if not all of the year's shoot production could be destroyed. This is especially true as giant panda hunt out surviving shoots the following winter. In these areas, only the periodic 'good shoot years', where many more than the average number of shoots is produced, allow the bamboo to survive.[10]

While the bamboo is under seasonal pressure from many species, the giant panda and red panda feed on the plant all year round (see Chapter 4). One other species relies on the bamboo throughout the year: the aptly named bamboo rat, *Rhizomys sinense*.

The genus *Rhizomys* comprises three species, found from southern China westwards across Indochina to Assam, and southwards to the island of Sumatra. Around 40 cm (15 ins) long, it is covered in a dense, soft pinky-grey fur, with small, piggy eyes and the most enormous set of yellow-brown 'buck teeth'. The short legs bear large digging claws. The bamboo rat is rarely seen above ground, preferring to spend its time in the extensive burrow system each family group excavates for itself around and beneath the bamboo stands. Large

Feeding on bamboo leaves is most common between the months of July and October

'mole-hills' around 40–60 cm (15–24 ins) in diameter and the occasional wilted bamboo stem are the only physical evidence of the animals' presence. One burrow system we examined in the Choushuigou area of Wolong measured around 175 m² (1880 square feet). The tunnels are about 15–17 cm (6–7 ins) in diameter, just enough to let the animals move easily through them, although they do widen in places to serve as nests (normally lined with bamboo leaves) and as latrines. The burrows lie some 15 cm (6 ins) below the surface. When excavated, the burrow systems are surprisingly extensive, with blind alleys and infilled older tunnels. There is anecdotal evidence that male and female bamboo rats may inhabit separate tunnel systems for most of the year.

The bamboo rats have developed specialised behaviour which they use to feed on their chosen food with the minimum of risk from predators. They tunnel close to a bamboo clump and, while still beneath the surface, use their enormous incisors to snip a stem from the rhizome. They then lie on their back or side in their tunnel and use their front paws to lead the stem into their continuously moving incisors, snapping away frenetically until most of the bamboo is consumed. From above ground, all that can be seen is the somewhat disconcerting sight of a bamboo stem sinking slowly beneath the surface of the earth. Very occasionally, bamboo rats will venture out at night to snip off a bamboo stem, dragging it back to their burrow and stopping up the hole with stones and soil.

Whether the bamboo rat and pandas compete for bamboo as a food resource is currently a source of much debate. On the face of it, they must compete. They both eat stems, and stems would seem to be a finite resource. It has been pointed out, however, that the activity of the bamboo rat is somewhat analogous to the human gardener's habit of pruning blackcurrants and other soft fruit – cutting out the old wood stimulates the plant to produce more fresh shoots. So the bamboo rat may be unwittingly doing the pandas a favour, thinning out the bamboo stands and stimulating the plant to produce new, thicker shoots. This is probably especially true of the umbrella bamboo, whose shoots the giant panda finds particularly palatable.

The bamboo can be classified into two main categories

according to the way in which they produce their shoots. Sympodial bamboo propagates itself as a clump, sending up shoots from around its circumference and so gradually spreading across the ground. By contrast, monopodial bamboo sends out runners in all directions, sending up shoots wherever conditions are favourable. In some areas stands of bamboo of vast total area can all derive from a single parent plant. In effect, the whole bamboo woodland is one enormous clone.

Clump-type bamboo tends to be found in tropical areas, such as the south of China. In panda country, high in the mountains, monopodial bamboo predominates, as it does over most of the temperate zone. In Wolong Reserve there are a total of seven species: *Phyllostachys nidularia*, *P. heteroclada*, *Sinarundinaria confusa*, *S. ferax*, *S. chungii*, *S. fangiana* and *Fargesia robusta*. Of these, only two, *Fargesia robusta* (umbrella bamboo) and *Sinarundinaria fangiana* (arrow bamboo), are important to Panda ecology.

Fargesia covers a little under 25 per cent of the area 'held' by all bamboo species. It is a lover of low altitudes, being found between 1600 m (5250 ft) and 2400 m (8000 ft) on the slopes and stripped plains of the mountains. Umbrella bamboo is quite a tall plant, with stems averaging 2.5 m (8 ft) in height (occasional specimens are over 5 m (16 ft). Stem diameter can be anything up to 2.5 cm (1 in) at the base, but average widths are just under 1.00 cm (0.4 ins). *Fargesia* grows in dense clumps, with thirty to forty stems crowding into a square metre (11 square ft). Because of this, and the way in which its long stems become tangled as they grow, moving through umbrella bamboo stands can be very difficult, at least for humans.

By contrast, arrow bamboo is slender, rarely thicker than 0.5 cm (0.2 ins), and much shorter than umbrella bamboo, with an average height of 1.4 m (4.5 ft). But what it lacks in height and girth, arrow bamboo makes up for in vigour. Stems are twice as dense as those of umbrella bamboo, seventy to seventy-five stems per m^2 (11 square ft), and its rhizomes are phenomenally active, sending out long runners that can colonise suitable habitat with surprising swiftness. In the Wolong area, arrow bamboo normally grows between 2600 and 3200 m (8500 and 10 500 ft). It grows thinly, if at all, in the more densely shaded areas, and can be entirely absent from ridges covered in rho-dodendron, but it flourishes almost everywhere else, standing in wide swathes of swaying stems that can blanket extensive areas. According to George Schaller's survey,[11] coverage in most areas averages between 50 and 60 per cent, and can reach 90 per cent in certain areas, so dense that it may seriously impede the regeneration of the forest over long periods, denying the seedling trees light. In the most densely growing areas not even moss can grow beneath the tightly packed stems. Evidence from other parts of China indicates that there is probably competition between the two species: in the Min Mountains of Sichuan, where arrow bamboo is absent, umbrella bamboo may colonise the slopes to a height of 3300 m (10 800 ft). This is a far higher altitudinal range than the species enjoys at Wolong and indicates that, where they coexist, the two species probably do compete for space.

Along with almost all other bamboos, the species at Wolong have another unusual feature that differentiates them from other members of the grass family – synchronous flowering. During most years the bamboo reproduces itself vegetatively, producing under-ground runners that send up new shoots to the surface at irregular intervals. This method has served the bamboo very well but by itself it is, in evolutionary terms, a dead end. To ensure long-term viability, sexual reproduction must take place at some point in the bamboo's lifetime so that different combinations of hereditary factors can occur. This ensures the genetic variety that allows a species to adapt to new conditions and new environments. All the grass family reproduces sexually, flowering and setting seed. But it is the bamboo's timetable that sets it apart from the rest of its kind.

Most 'normal' grasses flower every year, and the same is true for

Apart from pandas, the bamboo rat (Rhizomys sinense) is the only other species wholly dependent on bamboo for survival

a minority of bamboo species. Bamboos such as *Arundinaria wightiana*, *Arundinaria glomerulata*, *Bambusa lineata* and *Shibataea kumasasa* have never been observed flowering or seeding at greater than yearly intervals. These so-called iteroparous bamboos all grow to maturity and then flower, seed and die on an annual basis.[12] But most bamboo species 'hold back' their flowering cycles for relatively long periods of time. At regular intervals, varying with the species between thirty and 120 years, all the plants flower at the same time and then die. Distance does not seem to affect synchrony: in the late sixties the mainland Chinese giant timber bamboo, *Phyllostachys bambusoides*, seeded en masse in its homeland; transplanted bamboo of the same species also flowered at this time in Japan, Russia, England and the United States.[13] The cues that trigger such synchronous displays are not well understood.

Other plants, especially trees, display mass seeding: oak, beeches and some conifers have years in which an overabundance of seed is produced – for example, the well-known beech-mast. But these mast-seedings are derived from a population of adult trees of different ages, and they are capable of producing many mast-seedings over the course of their lifetime. As soon as such trees reach reproductive age they synchronise their reproduction with all the other trees in the area, using known environmental triggers, such as an exceptionally dry spring. By contrast, when bamboo sets seed all the plants that flower are exactly the same age, the environmental cues are not well known and the parent plants die after flowering. Only one other plant group can be said to emulate the bamboo's remarkable flowering pattern, the acanthaceous, genus *Strobilanthes*. Members of this group, such as the Indian 'niloo' (*Strobilanthes kunthianus*), are woody shrubs that grow as a dense group – sometimes carpeting a hillside for many square metres – persisting for a species' specific period of time before flowering and dying. There are a few other species – for example, the talipot palm – that flower and seed once before dying, but these trees do not grow in dense stands like the niloo and the bamboo.

The Chinese have known about the bamboo family's relations and the phenomenon of mass flowering for more than three millennia. The *Er Ya* defines the bamboo as a grass. In the *Classics of Seas and*

Mountains, a book dating from 770–256 BC, the authors record a sixty-year flowering cycle for an unnamed bamboo.[14] The *Shau Hai Jing* (*Record of the Natural World*) reported that: 'the bamboo will die in the year following its flowering'. Bamboos of economic importance naturally received the most attention. Other later chronicles give details of a 120-year flowering period for giant timber bamboo, noting that it flowered in the years AD 919 and AD 1114.[15] Modern records have confirmed the accuracy of the ancient reports, and added to the number of known flowering periods for a variety of bamboos. In most cases the bamboo's internal clock is not totally accurate. In Wolong the umbrella bamboo flowers every seventy to eighty years,[16] with the arrow bamboo having a shorter period of between forty-two and forty-eight years.

Bamboo mass flowering is nevertheless a fascinating, puzzling phenomenon. Why do the plants do it? What conceivable advantage can this frenetic burst of sexual activity followed by long quiescent periods have over the normal grass pattern of annual flowering?

Several conflicting theories have been advanced to account for mass flowering. It has been suggested that the energy 'saved' by not seeding can be channelled into additional vegetative reproduction. This is probably at least partly true; an increase in the number of underground runners that each plant can throw out should lead to that plant being able to compete more effectively with other plant species. The evidence for this, however, is mainly hypothetical and no real field work in this area has been done to underpin the theory.

Perhaps the most compelling theory for mass flowering is 'prey saturation': if bamboo flowered in an orthodox manner and produced a normal number of seeds, all these seeds would probably be consumed by the large number of seed-eaters that live in the forest. Bamboo seeds are at least as nutritious as the seeds of grains such as wheat; nor have they evolved the toxins that help protect the seeds of other plants. For a seed-eating species, the seeds are as defenceless as they are attractive. But, if the plant conserves its energy, husbanding its seed-producing potential for one enormous burst of sexual reproduction, it can swamp the seed-eaters by the huge weight of seed produced, and ensure that at least some of the seed is left to germinate.

The amount of seed produced can be prodigious. The seeds range from the size of a rice kernel to as much as 350 gm (12 oz). During mass seeding, the kernels can lie to a depth of up to 15 cm (6 ins) below the parent plant. A 33m² (40 yd²) clump of *Dendrocalamus strictus* produced around 145 kg (320 lbs) of seed. At 900 seeds to the ounce, this means that more than four and a half million seeds were set from this small clump of bamboo. Many birds and mammals take advantage of this bounty, everything from rats, mice and porcupines, through pheasants, doves and parrotbills, to Man. Where only a small 'island' of bamboo flowers synchronously the whole crop may be consumed and the species made locally extinct. More usually, however, the hordes of seed-eaters cannot cope with the superabundance of seeds.

Any bamboo in a given area that fails to flower at the 'correct' time will face severe retribution. Those few plants that flower too early will have their seed destroyed because it has not been produced in sufficient numbers to satisfy predators. Similarly, late-flowering plants will fall victim to seed-eating species that have been drawn to the earlier, heavier fall of seed, the survivors of which will, by now, have germinated and no longer be regarded as food by the seed-eaters. The very creatures that feed on the bamboo's seeds are responsible for maintaining synchronous flowering; the cycle is self-policing, once established.

The only species that could defeat this defensive stratagem, as it has defeated so many others, is Man. Humans counteract the mechanism that regulates synchronous flowering because they do not consume either the early- or the late-flowering plants. It is the main block of synchronously seeding plants that are preyed on. Fortunately for the bamboo, human seed collection is confined to a few scattered areas and does not seem to have a serious impact on the ability of the plant to flower in unison. Humans have probably harvested bamboo seed-fall for thousands of years, and in periods of famine the plant can substantially affect the chances of human survival. *Dendrocalamus* seeds were responsible for saving an estimated 35 000 people from starvation during a drought in the central provinces of India between 1899 and 1900.[17] Similarly, the Sasa bamboo of Japan was harvested in times of famine. In 1868, William Munro reported that two years before there had been:

> 'a general flowering of the bamboo in the Soopa jungles and ... a very large number of persons, estimated at 50 000, came ... to collect the seed. Each party remained about ten or fourteen days, taking away enough for their own consumption during the monsoon months, as well as some for sale.'[18]

If humans are the only species to defeat the mass flowering strategy, there is only one species that, potentially, can suffer irreparable harm from the bamboo's 'behaviour'. Rat and other species' populations may expand and diminish on the bamboo cycle of feast and famine, but the giant panda stands alone in possessing a painfully slow reproductive potential and in being entirely dependent on the bamboo for its survival.

There is a popular misconception that all the bamboo in a given area always flower at the same time. In many cases different bamboo species do not flower together, with only one species of bamboo in a certain locale blooming and setting seed in any one year. This seems to be because the 'alarm clocks' of different bamboo species are set for different times and it is only occasionally that the flowering cycles of two or more bamboo species coincide. Such synchronisation does occur occasionally, for example in the Min Mountains, where three different species of bamboo flowered simultaneously, with disastrous consequences for all wild creatures dependent on them. Even within a single species the bamboo tends to flower in a mosaic pattern. Most plants do flower, but certain stands continue to reproduce vegetatively long after the major flowering event. Altitude may also affect flowering times. In the Wanglang Natural Reserve in the Min Mountains, most of *Fargesia nitida* below 2900 m (9500 ft) flowered in 1975/76, but most plants of this species that grew above this elevation failed to flower, even five years after the bamboo lower down the mountain had set seed and died. It was not until 1982 that this higher altitude bamboo produced seed. So the picture is not quite as clear-cut as is popularly believed, especially when more than one bamboo species is available.

In a naturally wild habitat, untouched by Man, the giant panda can usually count on at least one other species of bamboo being available as a dietary fall-back. This species may not be as palatable or even as nutritious as the panda's favourite bamboo, but it can sustain the animal during the ten to fifteen years that it takes for the panda's preferred food plant to re-establish itself. Unfortunately, such habitat is nowadays becoming increasingly rare.

CHAPTER 4

DIET

At first sight the panda (both giant and red) is a paradox. Classified as carnivores (meat eaters) both species persist in acting like herbivores, feeding almost exclusively on plant material. The giant panda, in particular, has been described as an 'obligate grazer' on bamboo,[19] meaning that it is obliged to eat bamboo and that it cannot survive without it. Giant pandas in the wild are now known to eat at least twenty-six different plant species, but this figure is misleading. More than 99 per cent of the food they consume consists of bamboo. Less work has been done on the biology of red pandas' feeding habits, but it is certain that, as with the giant panda, bamboo forms by far the greater part of the animal's diet. In Wolong a sample of 332 droppings collected at all seasons showed that the red panda fed primarily (99.1 per cent by weight) on the leaves of the arrow bamboo.[20] During April and June when the bamboos produce shoots, the droppings revealed that only a small quantity of shoots (less than 5 per cent) were consumed. Unlike the giant panda which, as we will see, gorges itself on spring-time shoots and varies the proportion of leaves and stems consumed throughout the year (see Chapter 5), the red panda seems to be a specialist feeder, eating principally the leaves of the arrow bamboo. Individual red panda living at lower elevations, however, have been recorded as using the large succulent shoots of the bamboo, *Fargesia spathacea*,[21] some droppings being composed

*Red pandas often climb trees
in search of berries or the nests
of birds*

wholly of the shoots of this species. And other, usually anecdotal, evidence points to the red panda having a rather more varied taste in food than Johnson *et al*'s data suggest.

Don Reid, a World Wildlife Fund researcher, believes that red panda in Wolong eat *Sorbus* berries in season, while in other parts of their range the species has been observed robbing nests for eggs and chicks, catching birds and small mammals, and eating berries, acorns and blossom. Meat eating may be linked to the greater demands made on the animal during pregnancy; hunting and meat eating among captive animals does seem to peak during the female's gestation period.[22] In Washington Zoo the red pandas are recorded as having spent a good deal of their time stalking and catching birds. The red panda's eating habits seem to be far more flexible than those of the giant panda. The red panda's more catholic tastes seem to enable it to cope much better with the vagaries of life, including bamboo die-back. But however varied its diet, the red panda is still heavily dependent for its survival on bamboo, and without the plant it would certainly die. What is the reason for this reliance on a single plant species? Why should these two carnivore species have become vegetarian?

In a word, availability. The bamboo is one of the commonest plants in the conifer and mixed conifer and broadleaf forests that are the pandas' primary habitat. Bamboo is also evergreen. It may lose some of its leaves during the autumn and winter period but the green canopy of leaves can be seen pushing through the snow on even the coldest months of the year. For an animal looking for a plentiful regular food supply, the bamboo is ideal.

There is only one problem: the bamboo is a hard plant to love. It is not very palatable, at least to most species. Sambar and tufted deer, serow and golden monkey may occasionally feed on the leaves and tops of old shoots, and takin will also browse bamboo, but apart from the bamboo rat, and to a lesser extent the tree-dwelling rodent *Hapalomys*, very few mammals can stomach bamboo in large amounts. This can obviously work in the pandas' favour. For any animal that has found a way to survive on the plant, a lack of interest from other species is a positive advantage, because there is no competition for the food resource. The trick lies in 'learning' to survive solely on this unpromising plant.

Carnivores find it relatively easy to assimilate the foods they eat; protein is easily and quickly broken down to its constituent amino acids. Fats, too, invariably taken in during meat eating, are easy to digest. The alimentary canal of a carnivore is therefore a simple affair, with a single, sack-like stomach and relatively short intestines to absorb the nutrients. By contrast, the guts of herbivores are far longer. For example, a sheep's intestines measure twenty-five times the length of its body, a deer's fifteen times its body length. This compares with a figure for carnivores of between four and eight times their body length.[23] How does the giant panda fit into this scheme? Data are few, owing to the rarity of the animal, but on the basis of a study of four animals, the ratio of intestine length to body length averages out at 5.85, placing the giant panda plumb in the middle of the carnivore range. The red panda's ratio is similarly low, around four or five times the length of its body. Even the microscopic anatomy of the intestine testifies to the panda's carnivorous ancestry; the length of the intestinal villi — tiny finger-like protuberances which help increase the surface area of the intestine to aid absorption — are longer in carnivores compared with herbivores. Cats, for example, have villi measuring 960 μm as against 400 μm in an ungulate like the cow. The giant panda beats all these animals, turning in a figure of 1000 μm or more. In essence, then, both the giant and red pandas have retained the uncomplicated gut of a carnivore while feeding as herbivores.

But why should the guts of plant-eating animals be so much longer? The answer lies in the digestive difficulties posed by the foodstuffs they consume. The nutrients contained in plant material come in two very different 'packages': the contents of the plant cell, which are easily broken down to release their soluble nutrients; and the parts of the plant which maintain its structural integrity — lignin, cellulose and hemicellulose.

Simple chewing and swallowing will take care of the cell contents. Even carnivores can obtain a small amount of nourishment from plants in this way. But the tough fibrous components such as cellulose present a much more difficult problem. Neither carnivore nor herbivore can digest cellulose by themselves. But the plant-eaters have solved the problem by forging an alliance with micro-organisms that enable them to extract energy and nutrients from this otherwise indigestible plant material.

Micro-organisms break down both cellulose and hemicellulose by fermentation, and herbivores have evolved special refinements of their digestive system in order to provide a 'home' for these useful little microbes. Animals as diverse as hares, horses and rhinos have a caecum (a dilated pouch forming the first part of the large intestine) and a specially enlarged colon (large intestine) where the bacteria that feed on cellulose can live and where the food can be stored while fermentation takes place. This is the main reason for the length of a herbivore's gut: time is needed to complete the fermentation process, and a long gut means that the food can be retained in the body for a sufficiently long time to enable the process to be completed. The ruminant herbivores, cud-chewing animals like cows, deer and sheep, have provided an even more elaborate home for their bacterial guests. Typically, their stomachs are divided into four compartments, the rumen, reticulum, psalterium and the abomasum. After chewing, food passes down into the first two compartments where breakdown of the plant material starts. It is then regurgitated and rechewed before being passed through to the last two compartments, where bacterial fermentation is completed.

Pandas, however, eat plant material and seem to survive despite having a short gut and no cellulose-digesting bacteria to help them. And not only that: pandas have not chosen soft succulent plants to feed on, they have picked what must be one of the most nutrient-poor

The giant panda's rounded 'teddy bear' face is due to the huge jaw muscles needed to crush the hard, fibrous bamboo stems on which it feeds

and difficult plant foods to digest – bamboo. Yet the pandas have been around since the Early Pleistocene era; they have survived on a diet of bamboo for at least three million years. But how?

Despite the short length of their intestines, the lack of symbiotic micro-organisms and their classification as carnivores, both the red and giant panda show a number of evolutionary adaptations which are designed specifically to cope with their highly specialised diet.

Although the alimentary canal is short, the gullet of the giant panda is far tougher than that of most other mammals, including the red panda. This affords it some protection from the hard splinters of woody debris from bamboo stems. The wall of a giant panda's stomach is very thick, according to one researcher 'almost gizzard-like',[24] due in part to its extreme muscular development, itself an adaptation for squeezing and churning the roughly chewed bamboo fragments. The stomach and digestive tract have numerous mucous cells,[25] the copious production of mucus helping to guard against the cutting or tearing of the gut wall. Indeed, fresh panda droppings which we examined at Choushuigou were still coated with a layer of mucus. The red panda, who eats only the relatively soft bamboo leaves, shows none of these protective adaptations.

But it is in the structure of the skull and jaw that the pandas reveal the most obvious adaptations to a bamboo diet. Any animal that needs to eat large amounts of hard-stemmed vegetation needs three special talents: strong teeth, strong jaws, and enough muscle-power to use them. Primates like the gorilla exemplify this trend: the gorilla's cheek teeth are huge 'tombstones', flattened to give a large working surface to process the food, and embedded in a massive jawbone. The masseter muscles that work the jaw are enormous, so large that, at least in older male gorillas, the skull has a bony 'sagittal crest' running the length of the head to provide increased surface area for their attachment. The giant panda uses precisely the same method to accommodate its equally large masseter muscles. Along with the development of a sagittal crest, the panda's skull has become wider and deeper, allowing more space for attachment of the chewing muscles, and at the same time giving the animal that characteristic rounded, teddy-bear face, so beloved by humans.

The giant panda's jaw is extremely heavy boned, much heavier than that of a bear, the carnivore it most closely resembles, and carries teeth which, while fitting the general carnivore 'blueprint', show heavy modification for a herbivorous diet. The typical dental formula for a carnivore is I3/3 C1/1 P4/4 M3/4 meaning that in each half of the upper and lower jaw there are three incisors, one canine, four premolars and three/four molar teeth. The giant panda's dental formula is I3/3 C1/1 P4/4 M2/3 (although in some animals the first premolar may be absent), testifying to its membership of the carnivore club. The same is true of the red panda, with a I3/3 C1/1 P3/4 M2/2 dental formula. But this is only half the story. Most carnivores have carnassial teeth, modified premolars shaped like blades, which act as shears, allowing the animal to scissor off lumps of its prey neatly and efficiently. Both pandas and bears, whose omnivorous diet is made up of at least 75 per cent plant material, have lost their carnassial teeth, but it is the red and giant pandas that have taken this trend to extremes. Both the premolars and the molar teeth have been strongly modified for crushing and grinding bamboo. The posterior premolars and molars are wide and flat, their surfaces heavily ridged and cusped; the panda's teeth appear, superficially at least, more like those of cud-chewing species such as cattle and goats than the carnivore from which they evolved.

The panda's habit of holding food in its 'hands' as it eats is yet another example of an anatomical adaptation to the problem of feeding on bamboo. In Man and most other mammals the sesamoid bone is simply one of the many small bones that make up the wrist. In the giant panda, and to a lesser degree the red panda, the sesamoid bone has been specially enlarged to form a sixth digit. It protrudes from the animal's palm like a thumb, and like our own thumbs, it is opposable, allowing the panda to bring its 'thumb' against its first digit in a pincer-like movement. The dexterity afforded by this pseudothumb, combined with curved claws, used to hook culms towards the mouth, enable it to tackle bamboo stems and shoots with ease.

Strange as it may seem, the giant panda's large size may even be an adaptation to the low levels of nutrients provided by the

The giant panda's dextrous forelimbs allow it to process quickly huge quantities of bamboo shoots and stems

bamboo.[26] Big animals lose heat more slowly than small animals, owing to a decreased body surface area : body volume ratio.[27] Their metabolic rates are lower, meaning that they need to consume fewer calories to stay alive at any given temperature. If the giant panda were substantially smaller, it would find it difficult to feed on bamboo stems. Per kilogram of body weight, larger animals can also travel farther for the same amount of energy. The retention time of food in the gut is also increased, and excess energy is more easily stored in the form of fat.[28] All these arguments have been advanced by those who believe that the giant panda has evolved from a small, racoon-type animal, and that its resemblance to a bear is only superficial (see Appendix 2).

But however efficient these adaptations, the fact remains that most of the bamboo's energy is not available to both panda species. The pandas' digestion of bamboo is almost suicidally inefficient. The large teeth and strong jaws process the plant as efficiently as possible: the giant panda chews only briefly before swallowing while the red panda masticates its leafy food into a fine paste. But it is what happens after the food leaves the mouth that produces problems. Unable to digest cellulose and other structural carbohydrates in the bamboo's cell wall, and with its short gut giving a low retention time to extract whatever nutrients are available from the plant's cells, any animal would find it difficult to meet its nutritional requirements. To compound the problem, the nutritional content of bamboo is not very high (see Appendix 3, Figure 1). The giant panda therefore has to consume prodigious quantities of bamboo to meet its daily nutritional needs.

George Schaller and his co-workers weighed total daily droppings from wild giant pandas in Wolong. Using captive study animals and information from a variety of other sources, they were able to work out the amount of fresh bamboo a panda ate from the weight of droppings produced in any given time period. The panda Wei, tracked through snow during January, was estimated to consume just over 14 kg (30 lbs) of fresh bamboo in one day. An alternative method is to measure the number of stems eaten and the amount of debris remaining over a given foraging distance, and to extrapolate from this figure to obtain an estimate of total food consumed a day. Using this method the same animal, also during January, was found to have eaten about 17.8 kg (39 lbs) of bamboo, broken down as 7.4 kg (16 lbs) of stem and 10.4 kg (23 lbs) of leaves. Whether this discrepancy reflects an inherent inaccuracy in one (or both) methods is not known. It may simply mean that the amount of food giant pandas eat varies from day to day. In spring, when pandas start eating new umbrella bamboo shoots, the average weight of bamboo consumed can rocket. Zhen, a female weighing around 86 kg (189 lbs), ate on average 38.3 kg (84 lbs) of shoots a day, around 45 per cent of her body weight. On one day of particularly heavy consumption she ate 45.6 kg (100 lbs), rather more than half her own body weight in twenty-four hours.[29] Ruan and Yong, working in the Qinling Mountains of Shaanxi Province, also report a figure of 40–45 kg (88–100 lbs) of fresh bamboo shoots a day. In this area the food plant was the more massive *Phyllostachys* bamboo. Yong[30] mentions an almost unbelievable figure of 57 kg (125 lbs) or more a day of *Phyllostachys* shoots.

When feeding on succulent new shoots, the giant panda takes in more water than it needs; they rarely drink. Ruan and Yong[31] observed that one panda urinated a total of eight times in one day, testimony to the high water content of *Phyllostachys* shoots during the spring. At all other times of the year defaecation causes the elimination of more water than the giant panda can take in by eating bamboo. They are therefore constrained to drink at least once, and sometimes as often as four times a day. In the misty, stream-filled mountains that are its home, this is not really a problem, except perhaps during particularly cold spells when the small streams high on the mountain could be frozen solid. Then pandas may be forced to walk considerable distances in search of ice-free pools or streams. Pandas do not eat snow to obtain water; they would lose far too much body heat to make this behaviour worthwhile.

Water supply may be more important than most researchers realise. While filming in Wolong in 1991, we were shown areas of what seemed to be prime giant panda habitat, with abundant bamboo stands and level areas so beloved of the energy-conscious pandas. The

Giant panda resting while climbing slope. Steep inclines are normally avoided by pandas as they deplete energy reserves

nearest source of water, however, was just under a kilometre (0.6 miles) away. Giant panda had never been seen to set up home in this desirable residence. It was the opinion of the Chinese research workers that the energetic cost of walking this relatively short distance each day to obtain essential water was simply too great for the panda to bear. The animal's energy budget is so finely balanced that even a short regular walk can mean the difference between survival and death.

This hardly seems credible – until one looks at the daily calorie needs of the giant panda, and the amount of energy it is actually able to extract from its chosen food. George Schaller and his co-workers used the formulae derived by Moen in 1973 to estimate the energy expenditure of a hypothetical panda weighing 100 kg (220 lbs). They calculated that the basal metabolic rate or BMR (the amount of energy needed simply to rest quietly for twenty-four hours) was 2214 kilo-calories (approximately the same as for an office worker). To indulge in the normal panda activities of foraging, defaecating, and drinking (though not for social interactions, territorial behaviour or other social activities) cost the panda approximately an extra 40 per cent of its BMR. When such activities are taken into account, and a little more added for growth and reproduction, the total average energy require-ment for an adult panda is at least 3500–4000 kilocalories a day.[32] The same researcher calculated the giant panda's average daily intake of energy from bamboo to be between 4300–5500 kilocalories. The figures would be lower for those animals unable to feed on the more nutritious *Fargesia* bamboo shoots during the spring. If we take the higher energy requirement figure (4000 kilocalories) and the lower intake figure (4300 kilocalories, possibly lower) it is easy to see how finely balanced the species is between life and death.

This unique specialisation on bamboo is especially puzzling when there is another carnivore in the area, the Asiatic black bear, which finds approximately 75 per cent of its food from vegetable matter of various types. Bears feed on a wide variety of plants, over twenty-eight species in Tangjiahe, a reserve to the north of Wolong (see Appendix 3, Figure 2). In the spring, the bears feed largely on forbs such as the stalks of wild parsnip, *Anthriscus sylvestris*, shoots of

Rubus coreanus, and leaves and stalks of jack-in-the-pulpit (*Arisaema lobatum*). On occasion, bears will even sample bamboo shoots (*Fargesia scabrida* in Tangjiahe). As autumn approaches the bears change to berries such as the wild cherry (*Prunus* sp.), while by mid-September they are foraging mainly on nuts such as oak (*Quercus* sp.) supplemented by butternuts (*Juglans cathayensis*), hazelnuts (*Corylus* sp.) and a variety of fruits. Some of these plants are far more nutritious than the giant panda's staple fare of bamboo and, during the spring to autumn period, they are just as available.

Together with numerous researchers, we have seen giant panda climb trees with all the ease of a bear, and yet no one has ever observed a giant panda scaling an oak tree to take advantage of those highly nutritious nuts. Nor do any of the other plants that bears find palatable excite panda taste-buds. Schaller and his co-workers[33] report that giant panda will walk quickly through stands of nutritious wild parsnip (a favourite bear food) to feed on a nearby clump of much lower quality bamboo. Why, when the giant panda is balanced on a knife-edge of nutritional deficit which impinges on every aspect of its behaviour, does the creature literally walk past food that could make its life a lot less difficult? No one really knows but it may be that the millennia which honed the panda's behaviour and physiology into a specialist feeder also withered the animal's curiosity, its desire to know, to try out new things. The giant panda's brain seems to recognise only two categories of plant in its environment: bamboo (= food) and other vegetation (= non-food). That other plants may actually be better for it does not seem to have ever crossed the panda's mind. The animal is fixated on its food plant; it is a strategy that is fraught with peril in a changing world.

This fixation does not extend to animal protein. Given the panda's high bulk, low calorie diet, it is not surprising to find that the former carnivore has a taste for flesh. Following bamboo die-back in 1983 in the Qionglai Mountains, many pandas were lured to traps by mutton or goat cooking on open fires. The smell was apparently irresistible to them. Even in the absence of these human hand-outs, panda droppings do sometimes contain animal remains. George

Schaller and his fellow researchers discovered the hair of golden monkey in one panda's droppings, and the hooves, bones and hair of musk deer in another. In 1984, in Wanglang Panda Reserve, we were told that the giant panda ate mice and other rodents when it could catch them, a story apparently verified by the discovery of rodent remains in the guts of pandas from this area. Whether the pandas caught or simply scavanged these animals is not known, although scavenging is probably the most likely explanation. In the Tangjiahe Reserve, a wild panda studied by George Schaller chewed on the skin and leg bones of a long-dead tufted deer (*Elaphodus cephalophus*). But hunting is by no means out of the question. Having been chased on several occasions by irate pandas, we can vouch for the fact that they are capable of quite a turn of speed when they put their mind to it, perhaps enough to run down a young musk deer or smaller mammal. Villagers in Wolong informed researchers that they had seen a giant panda catch and eat a bamboo rat.[34] Perhaps most remarkable of all, a few pandas, like some lions or elephants, can turn 'rogue'. During our stay at Wolong Research Station we were shown a female giant panda whose favourite prey was goat. Where she had acquired this taste for goat flesh, or the skill necessary to catch and despatch a fully grown goat, was never discovered. Before she was captured and transferred to the research station she had managed to raid several farms and to kill and eat upwards of thirty-five goat and sheep.

Fresh or foetid, meat is undoubtedly a very welcome addition to the giant panda's normal, nutritionally meagre fare of bamboo stems, shoots and leaves. Meat provides a boost of protein and calories that the animal sorely needs, and the infrequent occurrence of animal remains in their droppings is almost certainly due to lack of hunting and scavenging opportunities rather than the panda's aversion to meat. Four of seven captive pandas in Wolong Valley immediately ate meat when it was offered them.

But the giant panda is not reliant on such infrequent bounty. Over the millennia, it has evolved to survive in a stable, unchanging environment where bamboo, though nutritionally inferior to most other foods, is nevertheless abundant and easily harvested. It must

Giant pandas are as adept as bears at tree climbing. Males use this high vantage point in territorial calling; females often see tree climbing as the only way to escape over-ardent suitors

feed hard and long simply to survive and reproduce, but that strategy has remained unchanged and served it well for at least three million years. To that extent, the species can be said to be 'well adapted' to its surroundings. But history has shown that, since the beginning of time, those species who gambled on stability have ultimately lost out in the game of life. By feeding almost exclusively on this one plant, the giant panda has put all its eggs into a single bamboo basket. Holes appeared in that basket as soon as Man began to alter substantially the panda's habitat.

CHAPTER 5

A DAY IN THE LIFE

L ike every other animal, the two panda species have had to establish a balance between energy intake and expenditure. Energy is rather like money in the bank: if the balance goes into the red, the outcome for a wild animal can be disastrous. There are few 'overdraft facilities' in Nature, and if expenditure exceeds income for any length of time, the result is weight loss, starvation and eventual death. Given the tiny surplus of calories that a diet of bamboo offers, the pandas must be particularly careful to make sure the energy budget balances.

Optimal foraging theory predicts that an animal will have evolved to make the best use of its time spent feeding. Behaviours such as locomotion, territoriality, courtship and mating all deplete energy reserves. Even so mundane an activity as defaecation requires energy, and the panda must allot no more than is necessary to each of these behaviours if it is to survive on its chosen diet. Just how the pandas spend their day and at the same time contrive to balance the energy books are the main subjects of this chapter.

Both giant and red pandas are notoriously hard to observe in the wild. Not only is the terrain in which they live difficult to travel, but the dense growths of bamboo and other vegetation allows even an animal as conspicuous as the giant panda to remain all but invisible to biologists trying to observe its behaviour. As the smaller of the

Precipitous, mist-sodden forests make studying the pandas in their natural habitat a nightmare

two, the red panda is especially hard to find and follow. Almost the only time human observers are aware of its presence is when it climbs a tree to sun itself or to sleep. And as soon as it descends the tree the red panda is swallowed up in the dense undergrowth. In the face of such problems researchers have had to resort to indirect means of determining panda behaviour. One method is to use the age-old techniques of the hunter, and to track the beasts and obtain information from their spoor and signs. Quite a lot of important information can be amassed in this way: how far the animal travels, how often it scent-marked or defaecated, what it fed on, the location of its sleeping place, etc. For example, biologists can estimate the time a panda stays at any site by reference to the number of fresh droppings at that site. As far as defaecation is concerned, the giant panda is as regular as clockwork, each dropping corresponding to a 'minute hand' of a biological clock, giving a fairly accurate assessment of the time spent in any one location. Supplementing tracking is a battery of high-tech equipment which is now *de rigueur* for any self-respecting field biologist: radiotelemetry in all its forms, from location devices, through radio-collars, to implants that monitor heart rate and activity. These techniques primarily depend on the ubiquitous chip and the miniaturisation of transmitting devices. The equipment is usually attached to a collar of some description which is fitted around the neck of the animal under study. Because they depend on radio waves to transmit the information to a receiver, all these devices work best in flat, open spaces; in mountainous, wooded areas the transmission can often be blocked by an intervening ridge or too dense a stand of trees, resulting in a loss of information, sometimes for days at a time. Recent transmitters have been aimed at satellite receivers which then transmit direct to a ground-station, effectively by-passing this particular problem.

So far, all our remote-sensing data on red panda behaviour are derived from a single female panda.[35] The panda concerned may be representative of the species, or she may be the panda equivalent of an eccentric whose actions lie at the fringe of 'normal' behaviour. No one knows. Whatever conclusions that are reached with regard to red panda behaviour on the basis of this one animal must be regarded as tentative at the moment. With giant panda we are on firmer ground. All told, upwards of five giant pandas have been radio-collared with a variety of instruments.[36] The red and giant pandas under study were fitted with a motion-sensitive mercury switch in the radio-collar each animal had bolted around its neck. When the animal is relatively motionless the radio-collar transmits at a rate of seventy-five pulses a minute. As soon as it begins to move the mercury switch is tripped causing an increase to 100 pulses a minute. The researchers also used the signals from the radio-collar to triangulate the position of the animals without ever going too close to the animal and perhaps altering its behaviour. As soon as the transmissions showed that the animal had moved on, the researchers descended on the newly vacated site to determine the animal's behaviour. This is an important precaution: should a panda know it is being watched it may 'freeze' for an extended period or alter its behaviour in more subtle ways, all of which will give the biologist a biased impression of the animal's activity budget. The single red panda and the five giant pandas studied by Johnson and his co-workers were monitored for activity at fifteen-minute intervals for seventy-two consecutive hours during the middle of each month.

The results indicate that, on average, giant pandas are active for around fifteen hours of every day, with the remaining nine hours of the animal's day spent resting. The giant panda seems to rest as and when the mood takes it; it will remain immobile for minutes or for hours. Normally, giant pandas look for somewhere to rest against when they search out a rest site (leaning against a tree or boulder requires less energy than sitting upright and so helps to save precious energy). Occasionally, the animal will shelter in a hollow trunk, or in a cave, especially during rainstorms or other inclement weather. Caves and tree hollows are probably the most sheltered locations available to wild panda, and it is these same sites that are chosen by pregnant females to give birth to their young. Although females of the species regularly construct breeding nests in such shelters as the birth season approaches, resting pandas never build nests, relying instead on their springy, oily coat to protect them from the cold and damp. Asiatic

Above: Because of their size,
red pandas feed mainly on
leaves at the base of bamboo

Opposite: Red pandas often use fallen logs
as pathways during daily travels
about their territory

black bear, who share the same habitat with the giant panda, often make nests from bamboo.

Resting giant panda either sit against a supporting tree or rock, or curl up on the ground, assuming a spherical shape. This reduces the surface area exposed to the air and so helps to conserve heat loss. They sometimes rest their cheeks on a fore- or hind-paw, using the limb as a pillow to insulate the head from the cold and often frozen ground. Red pandas use their tails to reduce heat loss, wrapping them around their bodies like fur stoles. Red pandas often sleep and rest in the fork of a tree. During fine weather this allows the animal to warm up quickly, as it can sun itself earlier in the day and without having to worry about being shaded by undergrowth. On cold days this habit probably saves heat by keeping the animal well away from frozen ground.

A red panda's resting sites are highly variable: a hollow stump, on top of a fallen log, tree stump or a tuft of dead grass. Rest site dimensions can vary from 23 cm (9 ins) to 51 cm (20 ins) in diameter. Sometimes, red pandas will dig hollows in snow or earth in which to lie up,[37] but generally speaking a rest site is not modified in any way – like its giant relative, red panda do not make nests in which to sleep. Of eighteen rest sites examined by Johnson in 1988[38] most were above ground level (average height of ten sites was in excess of 100 cm, or 39 ins) and one of these sites was in a tree at a height of approximately 13 m (42 ft). All rest sites were surrounded by droppings, although the pandas were not averse to resting atop a pile of faeces at five of the eighteen sites studied.

During its active periods the giant panda is primarily concerned with only one topic – eating. Of the giant panda's daily fifteen hours of activity, a colossal fourteen hours is given over to feeding, with only one hour spent on other maintenance activities such as excretion, drinking and grooming. By contrast, other carnivores normally hunt for extended periods and feed very rapidly, and even plant-eaters such as the impala spend no more than ten to eleven hours foraging. The only animals which feed as long, or longer, than the giant panda are non-ruminant herbivores which have few special adaptations for

digesting plant material.[39] The zebra, a non-ruminant species, feeds for 56 per cent of its day,[40] a figure which almost exactly parallels the 55 per cent of time the giant panda spends feeding. But, unlike most mammals, the giant panda can be found in an active state at any time of the day or night. Generally, activity (almost invariably feeding) reaches its lowest level in the morning, some time between 8.00 am and 9.00 am. It then rises steadily to an afternoon peak between 4.00 pm and 7.00 pm after which it declines rapidly to a low point around 10.00 pm. In summer and autumn this low activity level is maintained until it peaks the following morning, but during winter and spring the giant panda wakes early and there is a second activity peak during the hours of darkness, around 4.00 am to 6.00 am. Put simply, for most of the year the giant panda feeds for eight hours and sleeps for four hours during the day, then feeds again at night for another eight hours, after which it takes a second four-hour 'nap' before awakening to begin the cycle anew. Further study has revealed that the reason for this unusual behaviour can, as with most aspects of the giant panda's activity, once again be laid at the door of the bamboo.

Because the bamboo is hard to digest, a panda must eat often to keep its alimentary canal filled and allow an uninterrupted flow of nutrients into its body. But a panda's gut has a finite capacity, and the animal can only eat so much before the digestive system is filled. The capacity of a panda's stomach is around 4.5 kg (10 lbs) of bamboo, which happens to be the amount defaecated by a panda in five hours (bamboo travels the whole length of the panda's digestive tract in eight hours). So, any panda that sleeps more than four hours at a time will awake to a very empty stomach. Given the poor quality of the panda's diet and its need to maintain a steady trickle of nutrients into its system, an empty stomach is not the minor inconvenience it might be to most carnivores – it is a matter of survival. This explains the animal's need to work a shift of eight hours feeding and four hours sleeping through the day and night. The giant panda is quite literally constrained to feed around the clock.

Red panda are not so tied to a feed-and-sleep-and-feed routine. Work by Johnson[41] revealed an average active period of 36.5 per cent

Giant panda smelling bamboo leaves. The animal can apparently detect
subtle changes in the bamboo's nutritive value simply by using its nose

(eight hours) in every twenty-four-hour period. Statistically, the red panda is significantly less active than its larger cousin. The probable reason for the red panda's extra leisure time is its more efficient feeding behaviour.

Unlike the giant panda, which in the course of a year will consume bamboo stems, shoots and leaves, the red panda feeds exclusively on bamboo leaves. Leaves from the bottom of a bamboo stem are the ones most often taken; this is more the result of the small stature of the red panda than any dietary advantage in eating lower-growing leaves. The animal often walks along fallen logs during its daily travels and will then take the opportunity to sample leaves at the top of bamboo. The leaves are selected with great care, the red panda meticulously nipping off single leaves precisely at the junction of leaf and branch. Dead and partially dead leaves are rejected. By contrast, the giant panda's leaf-feeding method of collecting and eating handfuls of bamboo leaves invariably means that it ingests dead leaves. Dead leaves contain only 9 per cent crude protein, as opposed to 17.5 per cent for healthy green leaves.[42] And, once selected, red pandas chew their leaves finely, which probably makes more of the cell content available for digestion. The red panda's more selective feeding behaviour and meticulous mastication therefore brings the animal a much higher nutritional return per leaf than its larger cousin.

The red panda is essentially crepuscular (active at dawn and dusk) with two main activity peaks, one beginning before dawn and moving to a peak just after sunrise, and a second, shorter burst of activity towards dusk. Because it feeds solely on leaves, and bamboo leaves are available all year round, this pattern shows almost no variation with the changing seasons.

The giant panda's seasonal activity is almost as stable. But this stability hides a major difference in the behaviour of the two species. Because of its large size the animal cannot utilise its smaller relative's strategy of selective feeding and fine mastication of bamboo leaves. Collecting individual leaves and chewing them would simply take too long. Instead, the giant panda has opted for bulk processing. And despite, or perhaps because of this, the giant panda has become extremely sensitive to the mineral and nutritive content of all parts of the bamboo. The animal is constantly monitoring the leaf, stem and shoots of bamboo, weighing up the advantages of each, and making decisions to eat one part, or reject another. Using criteria we have yet fully to understand, it continually alters its behaviour to extract the best nutritional pay-off from bamboo. So, although the giant panda's activity budget remains fairly constant throughout the year (except for a drop in activity in September), what it actually does when it is active, especially its feeding behaviour, is far more varied compared to the red panda.

The giant panda recognises three ecological seasons in its food-year: spring (April to June), summer/autumn (July to October) and winter (November to March). During these three major divisions of the year the giant panda normally feeds on specific parts of the bamboo, or even changes its diet from one bamboo species to another.

In Wolong the panda's favourite bamboo is arrow bamboo. Pandas spend 85 per cent of the year above 2600 m (8500 ft) feeding on arrow bamboo from July all the way through to March. From July to October their food is almost exclusively the leaves of this species; no stems are consumed. By November, young stems are beginning to feature in the diet, along with leaves, a trend which continues until spring. At the end of this period, leaves suddenly drop out of the diet, the pandas selecting mainly old stems to eat. This is rather puzzling behaviour: leaves contain the highest levels of protein, followed by branches and stems. Arrow bamboo leaves also have the best balance of amino acids, which may be one reason why, over the year, they comprise so much of the panda's diet. Why, then, should the giant panda eschew protein-rich leaves in spring? The answer seems to be that the leaves become unpalatable to the animals at this time of the year because of a build-up of silica. Schaller[43] estimated the percentage of leaves in 339 droppings throughout the year, and compared these figures with the amount of silica present in the leaves of arrow bamboo over a twelve-month period (see Appendix 3, Figure 3). The graph clearly shows that giant pandas are aware of silica levels and reject leaves during those months when the silica levels are high.

Some arrow bamboo stems are consumed during spring, but most giant panda leave the higher elevations at this time and descend into the stands of umbrella bamboo. Spring is the time of maximum shoot production for most bamboo, and between May and June the giant pandas in Wolong feed almost exclusively on the emerging shoots of this bamboo species. Arrow bamboo shoots are found only as a casual item in the diet. So pressing is the urge to eat umbrella bamboo shoots that the pandas will leave their accustomed haunts to sample this seasonal fare. Why?

We have tried eating the shoots of both species and, as far as human taste-buds are concerned, there is nothing much to choose between them. But umbrella bamboo shoots are much larger and have more girth than those of arrow bamboo. They are also even higher in protein than arrow bamboo leaves, although the amino acid balance is not quite so good. From a panda's point of view it makes good sense to feed on umbrella bamboo: it is far more rewarding, in terms of energy, to eat thick juicy shoots than thin juicy shoots. With both, energy must be expended to search for, pick and process the shoot. The umbrella bamboo shoot obviously provides a far higher ratio of energy input to energy output than its less robust relative. That this is true is shown by the animal's behaviour within such a stand. Giant pandas do not feed randomly on the shoots. Generally speaking, they leave shoots less than 0.9 cm (0.3 ins) in diameter, and concentrate on shoots with diameters of 1.00 cm (0.4 ins) or more. They also search for food along the edge of the umbrella bamboo clumps, where the extra light allows plumper, juicier shoots to grow. Height is also important; pandas tend to ignore short shoots less than 25 cm (10 ins) high. The 'bigger shoots provide more energy' explanation probably partly explains this behaviour, but the reasons behind the rejection of short shoots are a little more complex.

When they emerge from the ground umbrella bamboo shoots are covered by a protective hairy sheath which is unpalatable and painful for humans to consume. Giant pandas seem to feel the same way. The creature takes pains to remove the sheath from the shoot before eating, normally by holding the shoot aslant in its mouth and tearing the sheath off with a pulling and twisting motion of its paws and mouth. But sheath removal is a relatively costly energy activity. It turns out that the shoots the giant pandas select to feed on give the best return; in short shoots the ratio of (digestible) core to (indigestible) sheath is 1:2 by weight. This ratio is reversed with long shoots, with core outweighing sheath by a healthy 2:1. In this, as in every other aspect of its activity budget, giant panda behaviour is finely honed to maximise food intake and minimise energy expenditure.

Feeding on umbrella bamboo shoots – note the pale-coloured discarded sheaths littering the feeding site

CHAPTER 6

PANDA SOCIETY

Over the past 20 years it has become clear to biologists that the social organisation of a species is flexible and not an immutable set of behaviours. It depends on local environmental conditions and the type of habitat in which the study was carried out. Biologically speaking, a species cannot be described as being, say, 'solitary and territorial', full stop, without adding 'in this or that particular habitat'. This is especially true of carnivores. And despite the fact that the giant panda is an atypical carnivore, it is still important to consider the results of any panda study with this in mind.

A graphic example of behavioural flexibility is the spotted hyena, *Crocuta crocuta*, in Tanzania. In Ngorongoro Crater, where the movements of the hyena's main prey, gazelle and wildebeest, are confined, and where there is intense competition among the hyenas for food and space, ecologist Hans Kruuk found that hyenas are organised into highly territorial clans of between thirty and eighty animals to defend the limited and localised food resource.[44] The boundaries of the territories are patrolled regularly and marked frequently. But on the open plains of the Serengeti, further west, where the same prey migrates over large areas, the hyena lives a solitary free ranging life and is not territorial, because it is forced to follow its food. The main directive behind these two different social set-ups is the pattern of food distribution, whether patchy or dispersed. Such behavioural flexibility gives individuals the best chance of survival because it allows them to respond to local conditions.

The social organisation of giant pandas has been studied in one location only – a 35 km² (13 square miles) area in Wolong Nature Reserve – so our knowledge of this particular aspect of giant panda biology derives solely from this area.[45] It is unlikely that giant panda biology is different in other populations because, unlike the red panda, the type of habitat it lives in – a mixed forest of bamboo, evergreens and deciduous trees – does not vary much from one part of its range to another. All the same, it is as well to bear in mind that in certain, as yet, unstudied parts of its range giant panda biology might be different.

To obtain a profile of the giant panda's social organisation, Schaller and his colleagues posed the following questions: Is the panda solitary or social? Do individuals defend their home ranges, in other words, are they territorial? How do individuals use their home ranges, i.e., what are their movement patterns like? What are the giant panda's population statistics (or 'dynamics') – namely, the proportion of males to females, adults to sub-adults and infants, the degree of survival in each of these age groups, birth rates and overall death rates, and age at sexual maturity? To answer these questions, Schaller and his team set out to monitor as many giant pandas as possible. They managed to trap six (three males and three females) and snared one (a male) using chunks of sheep or goat meat as bait. They radio-collared the animals and plotted their movements, levels of activity, etc, for eleven months. This information was combined with data from indirect observations – spoor, droppings and other signs such as bark scratching and tree biting.

Once all the information had been collated, the first thing that was obvious was that giant pandas were solitary animals. This confirmed the early reports of Western collectors and hunters over large parts of its range. Being solitary does not mean that one's social organisation is any less complex or organised than that of a social creature. It simply means that individuals live by themselves as opposed to living in groups. They still get involved in relationships with neighbours, mates and rivals for mates. And even in solitary mammals, individuals are obliged to come into direct contact with each other at least twice in their lives. Males and females must meet to court and mate, and infants need to remain with their mothers for however short a period until they can cope on their own.

The Wolong research team discovered that the giant panda is not territorial. It has a clearly defined home range in which it spends all its life and which contains all the resources it needs to survive: food, mates, nesting sites and shelter, but it does not defend this area from other animals of the same species. Individuals neither patrol nor scent-mark the borders of their home ranges, nor do they engage in any direct territorial confrontations. Females do not share any of their home ranges with other females, but the home range of each male overlaps considerably with those of male neighbours and with those of three to four females. The overlap between male ranges can be so great that neighbouring ranges may overlap with those of the same females (see Appendix 4, Map 1).

What makes the giant panda non-territorial? There are probably at least two reasons. First, there is really no need to be territorial as the most important resource, food – in this case, bamboo – is abundant and so does not need to be defended. Second, bamboo is so nutritionally poor that finding and eating sufficient to sustain life is arduous enough without adding another energy-expensive activity such as territorial patrol. Because they do not have this extra energy burden, giant panda males can afford to have home ranges big enough to encompass several female ranges. The only alternative would be to defend a small territory, but this would not only mean fewer potential mates, it might mean none at all if a higher status male were to oust him. Having a virtually communal home range rather than a freehold

The Wolong ('Sleepy Dragon') Mountains – typical panda country

territory means that neighbouring males may also share the same resident females and so the males compete with each other for females. The males that come off best are those of high rank. Rank is based on size, age and experience, and is established through olfactory communication long before the start of the breeding season.

The giant pandas of Wolong do not move about their home ranges to any great extent. A resident, especially a young lower status or inexperienced animal, will visit as little as 10 per cent of its home range in any one month, and some parts are visited only rarely. This is atypical of carnivore behaviour, a feature of which is extensive foraging movements within home ranges. The giant panda's strategy here is not altogether surprising as the species is a carnivore only taxonomically. In practice, they are herbivores. The only time they need to move extensively is during bamboo die-back, when migration to other food areas is forced on them. Males have no favourite area, or core area, and tend to use more of their range than females. Females concentrate their activities within a core area (30–40 hectares, or 74–99 acres) which contains most of the resources they need. A female will share her core area with adult males only, because although she does not patrol the boundary of her core area, this zone is sacrosanct and sub-adults and other females are regarded as trespassers.

Foraging movements depend on where the best available food is in any season. Spring is an active time for giant pandas, when they make good use of their home ranges in search of stands of umbrella bamboo. In spring 1981, a poor season for the shoots of this bamboo, one of the radio-collared females in Schaller's study, Zhen, actually crossed over Wolong Valley to the opposite slope in search of food. Not only was this a long journey for a giant panda but a very risky one as well, across a cultivated, populous valley lacking any cover. The following two years were good food years and Zhen made no attempts to cross over again.

Summer is when pandas are at their laziest. They make many fewer excursions around their home ranges and loll about eating long picnics of bamboo. Things hot up again in the winter, a time of dwindling food supplies and, for males, the period leading up to finding a mate. During this period, adult males use more than half of their home range and are busy keeping tabs on the females within it. Significantly, sub-adult males, which are not yet ready to breed, use less than half of their ranges during this period.

Female home ranges are located in the best areas. Best for food, for microclimate, for nesting sites and for foraging. This translates into a number of habitat features: almost continuous cover of arrow bamboo; south- and west-facing exposures, where snow does not persist for as long as on other inclines; gently sloping ground, which avoids strenuous climbing and saves precious energy; hollow trees or caves for dry, secure den sites; and a well-wooded area with an almost continuous forest canopy. In open areas bamboo grows more densely than beneath a canopy and the stalks are drier and tougher. They also tend to be stunted and more leaves die in winter, which reduces the nutritional content. A good canopy supports less dense, more nutritious bamboo groves and also gives shelter from the rain and snow. The large trees that form the canopy also provide den sites.

The main imperative for a male is to maximise access to potential mates, which means home range overlap with as many females as possible. Sub-adults draw the short straw in this situation. They have to make do with less than ideal living quarters. In the Wolong study two sub-adults that had formed a loose acquaintance, Long and Ning, shared a home range on a steep hillside cut by many ravines and almost denuded of trees. They concentrated their foraging in and around the remaining forest patches rather than attempting to exploit the open slopes. This shows that open habitat is clearly not preferred and implies a level of competition between adults and sub-adults for resources.

By carnivore standards, giant pandas are modest landowners. Home ranges are small, varying from 3.9 to 6.4 km² (1.5–2.5 square miles), and female ranges are almost the same size as those of their male neighbours. This is quite unlike the situation in large carnivores such as the black bear and grizzly bear, where male home ranges may be several times larger than those of females and where males particularly frequent all parts of their home ranges.[46] The reason for

Giant panda in an aggressive threat posture – the black ears contrast sharply against the white fur of the panda's back, giving it a 'four-eyed' appearance

this difference, no doubt, lies once again in the giant panda's limited menu. It may be that there is a limit to the size of land that a male can monitor on his low-nutrient diet. He is constrained to spend most of his time searching for, and eating, bamboo. As with most other mammals, the size of a giant panda's home range changes as the individual matures. Young pandas start off by sharing their mother's home range. Then, after they part company with her, they may make exploratory trips into new areas, sometimes travelling as much as 14 km (8.5 miles) in a day (the norm is usually 2 km (1.2 miles) a day) to look for the best available area. Once the choice has been made and they are ready to mate, the young adult will settle down into a home range of its own.

Face to face encounters are rare in giant panda society. But with such extensive overlap between home ranges, pandas are bound to meet up occasionally with one another. Most encounters are male-male or male-female encounters. The only female-female associations are between a mother and her infant daughter where the relationship is one of provision and protection on the part of the mother and dependence on the part of the daughter. In male-female encounters, the subject is sex and the outcome is courtship and mating. In male-male meetings the 'conversation' is not about territorial boundaries, it is purely about rank, about who is likely to take precedence for a female's favours. The outcome of meetings between males is only very rarely aggressive because that is risky and wasteful. More usually, it is mutual agreement about which of the two has a higher rank and therefore who should give way to whom. Older, bigger males with more experience command higher status but in time they will slip down the hierarchical ladder as age takes its toll.

Although the giant panda is solitary, it is not antisocial. No solitary species is. Exchanging information is as important as it is in social species, to integrate the members of a population and to space them out. All animals require reliable news bulletins on who is doing what and where. Because pandas seldom meet, close-contact visual signals are not the norm and are not very well developed, but they are important when face to face confrontations occur. Most visual options are ruled out for the giant panda. For example, the contrast between the black ears and the white crown is obvious and might, at first sight, be expected to play a part in visual communication, but the lack of ear movement, whatever the emotion of the animal, makes this a non-starter. The black nose and lips are prominent, but the panda's face, with its short muzzle, is incapable of much expression. The eye patches act like eyeshadow and mascara and make the panda's eyes look huge but the eyes themselves also lack expression. The short tail can hardly qualify as a display organ and the fur is short without a size-enhancing erectile crest. All in all, not a very useful set of visual hardware. What face to face visual communication there is is done through body postures with the help of the panda's striking markings.

The first of these is the threat posture. A giant panda faces its opponent and stares at it with lowered head so that the ears stand out against the white fur of the shoulders and duplicate the eye patches. The animal may then bob its head up and down for good measure. If emotions escalate, pandas will swat each other with their forepaws and lunge at or grapple with each other with paws and muzzle. They may do this while squatting, standing or leaning into each other on their hind legs. Schaller observed that:

'If one turns away, the other may bite nape or shoulder and shake its head while doing so. The attacked animal may be pushed or roll onto its side or back, all four legs flailing, while the other straddles or drapes itself over the fallen opponent, mouthing and pawing, and sometimes biting with or without a head shake.'

To convey a non-combative stance, the animal plays down the four-spot effect of the eyes and ears by averting its head or, in an even more submissive stance, will drop its head between its shoulders and cover its eye patches and muzzle with its forepaws. During mating, a female will go further in submission and rest the top of her head on the ground so that there is not a hint of confrontation. A non-aggressive panda may also imitate its actions in infancy and roll on its back as if in invitation to play.

What the giant panda lacks in facial expressiveness it more than makes up for in an impressive repertoire of calls.[47] These enhance the language of body posturing. There are about eleven distinct sounds that a giant panda emits, although there are gradations between most of them. Three of these, the huff, snort and chomp, are 'non-vocal', which means that they are not produced with the larynx; they are simply forcible expulsions of air modified by the animal's soft palate, throat and lips. By far the loudest and most intimidating of calls, to humans and pandas alike, is the roar. This call conveys aggressive threat at the highest level and is also used to locate the caller. It is a sound most often heard through the shifting mists of an April dawn when males are fervently seeking a mate. Both males and females will roar at each other from a distance and the sound is made to travel even further by calling out from the lofty heights of a tree. Females will also roar at courting males when they are not yet ready to mate and cannot be bothered by the males' persistent attentions. Roars are also emitted if two pandas quarrel during chance encounters. Another unambiguously aggressive call is the growl, which is not unlike that of a dog's. As with the roar, the growl is emitted by the more assertive individual and is often given with a moan.

The huff, snort and chomp are the calls of an apprehensive animal and are usually given in combination with the honk – for example, snort-honk, snort-chomp-honk, and huff-snort-chomp-honk. The huff and snort are more aggressive than the chomp, which is more a defensive call, uttered in anxiety. The chomp is also known as 'jaw-clapping' and is a repetitive sound consisting of a click, as the teeth are brought together, and a smack made partly by the animal vibrating its lips as it expels air through its mouth. Honking and, to a greater extent, squealing, convey distress and apprehension, a clear absence of aggressive intent. A sub-adult or low status panda will honk or squeal when threatened or attacked by an adult or higher status adult.

The other calls, the moan, bark and yip/chirp, signal increasing states of excitement. A panda may utter these in a variety of complex combinations and also with snorts, squeals and bleats. Their function depends on their context. In direct confrontations – for example, during courtship, when startled or when meeting casually – the moan, bark and yip may convey a mild warning against further interference and are essentially non-aggressive. Pandas also use the loud, audible moans and barks as long-distance calls, to advertise themselves, particularly in the mating season. The moan is a very variable call, described by the Schaller team as: 'ranging from a sharp hoot and softly repeated bu-bu-bu to a low-pitched moo, whiny groan, and long-drawn moan rising and falling in pitch, some, plaintive, others harsh'. Facing another individual, a panda will sit or stand with lowered head and moan with mouth open or closed, or alternately open and close it. The chirp may also function as a social call during courtship and, with squeals, may also be used to draw attention to the caller.

The only call that lacks any aggressive or anxious undertones is the bleat. Sounding like the bleat of a goat, it is entirely friendly. It is a close-contact call uttered in the way of reassurance by courting and mating couples. The bleats of a panda are peculiar to that individual and so it probably works alongside smell to help individuals recognise one another.

One sound that is entirely confined to infant pandas is the squawk which can be short or long and drawn out. Young pandas make this sound when cold or uncomfortable and the more distressed they are the greater the pitch of the call.

In mammals short-distance calls focus attention on the caller, who then conveys further information by means of facial expressions, postures and movements. The giant panda's face does not lend itself to subtle expressions and its dense bamboo environment means that body posturing is not as useful as it could be. Detailed information on emotional state is conveyed through the complex combination of calls and intermediate sounds a panda makes during an encounter. Judging by the complexity of the calls – combinations of sounds such as moan-growls and roar-squeals, the merging of one call into another to produce a continuous signal, and calling at different intensities – a giant panda experiences rapid shifts in emotions. For example, during any one encounter, it can shift through apprehension, defensive threat and offensive threat. Pandas are particularly vocal carnivores when interacting, and Schaller has suggested that their need to communicate emotional and physical information is made all the more acute by the fact that meetings are infrequent.

Vocalisations are important in giant panda society but they are not the panda's everyday language. Routine news broadcasts are made by leaving scented messages and visual posters at traditional spots. These are the answerphones of giant panda society and without them chaos would ensue. Odours applied to solid objects persist and convey messages long after the communicator has left the site. They are an especially important means of communication for solitary species which seldom meet to exchange visual and vocal signals. Scent enables several pandas to exchange information without having to congregate, a facility of immense importance for a species which needs to space out its members. Scent is so important for social integration that animals will leave tell-tale trails which give away their whereabouts to their predators, and some carnivores, in turn, sacrifice part of the surprise element in hunting because of their own distinctive smells. The response of an individual receiving a message depends on its sex, its status in society, its reproductive condition and also its previous contacts with the depositor.

So what information do smells contain and where are they produced? Droppings and urine probably contain information on an individual's identity and perhaps its sex, and food remains simply say 'I've been here', but the most important information carrier is scent. This is a dark substance that is produced by the glands around the anus and genitals. These 'perfume factories' are engaged in full-time production of strong-smelling scent. Scent conveys information on the sex of the depositor, its age, how long ago it left the area and, if it is a female, whether it is in oestrus and ready to mate, and also the extent of male rivalry. Every individual has an odour print specific to itself and so the scent deposit also functions as an identity card.

Receiving an olfactory message requires a mere sniff, but leaving a message is rather more involved and is perhaps the most energetic of giant panda activities. A giant panda will deposit scent on the ground, a tree stump or log by squatting and rubbing its anal gland on the surface, using its bushy tail as a paint brush. Pandas will also scent-mark taller objects such as trees, particularly conifers, which have rough barks that perhaps allow scent to adhere better and last longer. To scent-mark a tree, a panda will either squirt urine onto it or rub scent from its anogenital glandular area. It does this by backing up onto the tree and raising its tail. A panda rarely does both actions – urination and rubbing – in any one session but it usually combines either with trunk clawing. While marking, the depositor may shake his head or bob it up and down. On occasion, a panda will leave its message at a greater height to increase the dispersal area of the scent. To do this, it will either cock its leg against the tree or, more rarely, do a handstand. Despite its size and bulk, it manages this by backing up against the tree and 'walking' up the trunk with its hind legs. Frequently marked conifers are easy to spot. An observer's eyes are drawn to a dark, smooth area where the scent and urine have been applied and, above that, an area lightly scoured by claws. This visual part of the signal is useful because it lasts longer than the scent deposit, which in turn lasts longer than the urine signal. Schaller could smell this urine from about 5 m (16 ft). It is especially musky, unlike normal urine, and Schaller thinks that it may contain, in males, a secretion from internal glandular tissue around the tubes that lead from the testes. Unlike the red panda, giant pandas do not leave droppings at scent posts. A giant panda defaecates at rest sites and wherever it happens to be at the time.

At Wolong, pandas mark only about 20 per cent of their scent kiosks on a regular basis. The rest are maintained infrequently. Territorial animals tend to concentrate their scent-posts around the perimeter of their territories like 'keep-off' fences, but for non-territorial creatures like the giant panda scent-posts are more effective concentrated along busy routes used by residents and transients. Ridges, low passes and spurs projecting into valleys are all examples of such busy traffic areas. These motorways of the panda world are areas where the bamboo is at its least dense, allowing for easy, unencumbered travel.

There is no time of the year when giant pandas do not mark and it is the males that monopolise this activity. Wei, an adult male in the Wolong study, marked forty-seven trees over a distance of 7113 m (23 000 ft) during the winter of 1981–82. The biologists tracked the female, Zhen, for 1868 m (6000 ft) during the same period without finding so much as a claw mark. Males mark throughout the year, although efforts are stepped up in the mating season when marking is directed at females. For the rest of the year, marking is directed at other males in order to maintain mutual distance and to ascertain rank.

Beside clawing, pandas use other visual posters to draw attention to their presence – bark stripping, tree biting, ground pawing, and rubbing and rolling – but these are not used very often and are probably minor communication aids. Claws, teeth and body fur are the pen and ink of such poster making. Bark stripping involves gnawing and scraping lumps of bark off trees, particularly conifers. In tree biting a panda usually bites a sapling in two. Most tree biting is done in April, the mating season, and is probably the work of males wanting to be noticed, but females do, on occasion, use saplings to line their maternity dens.

Claw marks higher up a tree indicate that an animal has actually climbed the tree, an activity which both males and females engage in during the mating season, the females to escape the attentions of their suitors, the males to pursue potential mates and to use the tree as a soap-box when advertising their presence by calling.

In ground pawing, a panda will brush away a 30–40 cm (11–15 ins) in diameter patch of soil or snow, usually on a rise or at the base of a tree. Rubbing and rolling involves just that – rubbing and rolling the body on the ground or against rocks and other surfaces. In ground rolling, soil is rubbed over the body and the vegetation is trampled and covered in the panda's body scent.

To obtain information on an animal's population dynamics – its density; the relative proportion of different age classes; birth and death rates, etc – requires years of research. The population also has to be big enough to make the figures valid. For a large, wide-ranging carnivore, this usually means tens rather than hundreds. Even so, the

*Bark-stripped trees are a form of visual communication which alerts
other pandas to an individual's presence in the area*

Wolong study involved only eighteen animals, a small population by any standards, but it is enough to give us some idea of the giant panda's population dynamics. The data are based on radio-collared animals and from direct and indirect sightings. Panda density in the 35 km² (13 square miles) study area was about one animal per 1.9 km² (0.7 square miles), or one animal per 1.24 km² (0.5 square miles) if we consider only the twelve residents and only the 15 km² (6 square miles) of *Sinarundinaria* bamboo where the pandas spent most of the their time. As a panda need only about 0.5 km² (0.2 square miles) of *Sinarundinaria* to live on indefinitely, it is clear that the Wolong environment could actually support more than twice the number of pandas it does. In other words, food is not a limiting factor on panda numbers in Wolong. The other factors, principally human interference, will be discussed in Chapter 9.

Knowing the relative proportion of different age classes in a population is useful in assessing the health of a population – whether it is stable, increasing or declining. Too high a proportion of young animals and too few adults of breeding age could indicate that there are not enough adults to sustain population levels. Equally, too few young animals indicates that the breeding adults are for some reason not producing young. Schaller and his colleagues identified three age classes in the Wolong population of giant pandas: infants (birth to 1.5 years, the age at which they leave their mothers); sub-adults (1.5 years– 5 years); and adults (5 years plus). The relative proportion of the Wolong age classes was two infants; four independent sub-adults; and twelve adults (seven males and five females). The fact that there were six animals below breeding age indicated steady recruitment in the Wolong population.

Giant pandas reach sexual maturity at around $5\frac{1}{2}$ to $6\frac{1}{2}$ years of age whatever their sex. Females often come into oestrus before then but they are not behaviourally ready to mate. The average litter size is 1.7, a figure derived from thirty-seven litters born in captivity between 1963 and 1983. Females often give birth to twins, but sometimes only to one and, occasionally, to three cubs. One cub of a twin usually dies as the female is only able to feed one baby but, surprisingly, wild females will occasionally try to rear both infants which perhaps suggests better nutrition in the wild. If an infant dies (or, in captivity, is removed) before it is 6 months old, the female may come into oestrus again in the spring. Normally, though, a baby panda will remain with its mother for one and a half years, which means that in the following year's mating season, its mother's oestrus is suppressed and mating does not occur. The maximum reproductive rate for the giant panda is therefore about one young per female every two years.

Large carnivores of giant panda size, such as bears, live for about twenty to thirty years. Information on giant panda longevity is sparse as most zoos have not kept giant pandas for this length of time, but one female in Beijing Zoo died around 30 years of age and another female in Nanjing Zoo lived for twenty-nine years. Pandas in zoos outside China have a much shorter lifespan, seldom surviving longer than fourteen years. If the giant panda is like the grizzly bear in having no menopause, i.e., if females can bear young for as long as they live, then we can calculate the maximum number of young a female can raise. Assuming she has her first baby at 6 years of age and rears one young every two years, then by the time she is, say, 24 years old, she will only be able to raise nine young at the very most.

Judging from the rearing success of Zhen in Wolong this birth rate is, in reality, probably a good deal less. Zhen gave birth to three babies during a four-year period but only one seems to have survived, and the fate of even this one was uncertain at the time Schaller wrote his report. Another female called Han was lactating just prior to her capture and yet there was no evidence of an infant in subsequent months. There are many reasons for infant death, some of them due to the mother herself if conditions in captivity are anything to go by. One captive female crushed her offspring, while another partially ate one of her cubs soon after birth. In the wild, females have to leave their young unattended for long periods in order to feed and this means the little ones are open to attack from such predators as leopards, golden cats, yellow-throated martens and weasels. Even when infants are old enough to leave the den they are still small enough to be vulnerable to attack from the larger predators and this may be true even of sub-adults up to about $2\frac{1}{2}$ years of age, weighing about 50 kg (110 lbs). Cubs, especially those still taking milk, may also starve if they become separated from their mother among the dense stands of bamboo. They depend on her for a milk supplement (during the weaning period) and for helping them to find the right bamboo.

Available information is too sparse to say anything about the mortality rates of giant panda populations. Although the young are vulnerable to predators there is nothing to indicate that this is a major mortality factor. Little is known about giant panda diseases but while some parasitic infestations, such as roundworm, may weaken members of the older generation and kill them, there has been no evidence of major outbreaks or serious levels of illness. All of these pressures pale into insignificance in the face of the biggest killer of giant pandas – Man. Humans kill pandas for their skins, sometimes using traps set for musk deer. But even worse is the constant war of attrition waged against panda habitat in the name of timber products and ever more crops. Loss of natural habitat produces a slow decline in panda numbers as well as regular sharp losses during mass bamboo die-backs, when pandas in areas disturbed by Man have few alternative food sources.

There have been no studies of red panda in the wild, equivalent to the long-term one carried out on giant pandas. To date, there has been only one published field study in China (in Wolong) and one in Langtang National Park in northern Nepal.[48] The Wolong study was based on one panda that was radio-collared after being caught

Bark-stripped trees are a kind of visual communication which alerts other pandas to an individual's presence in the area

accidentally in a giant panda trap and followed for nine months. The Nepal study drew on observations from nine pandas. Information on spacing patterns and social organisation is therefore sparse and data on communication comes almost exclusively from animals in captivity. What seems to be clear, however, is that, like the giant panda the red panda is solitary, but territorial with individuals holding exclusive, non-overlapping territories. Population density in the Lantang study area is approximately one panda for every 3.9 km² (1.5 square miles). Males frequently patrol the perimeter of their territories but females spend most of their time in their core areas. Both males and females concentrate scent-posts along the periphery of their home ranges rather than just along well-travelled routes, like the giant panda. Females choose high-quality ranges, areas well supplied with food, cover and nesting sites. Males, on the other hand, are more interested in defending areas that contain as many mates as possible.

Male red pandas in the Nepal study area had much larger home ranges than their female neighbours (1.7–9.6 km², or 0.6–3.7 square miles) compared with 1.0–1.5 km², or 0.4–0.6 square miles), a pattern that is in keeping with other carnivores but one that contrasts with the giant panda set-up. The territory of the Wolong female was larger (3.4 km², or 1.3 square miles) than that of her Nepalese sisters. Males are generally more active than females and increase their territories during the winter months by as much as 74 per cent, both in response to leaner times and to breeding activity.

Red pandas differ from giant pandas in their movement patterns. They travel about the same distance every day to forage (about 1.75 km, or about 1 mile as the crow flies), but red pandas do not use as much of their home range over a given period, tending instead to concentrate their activities in certain specific patches of their home ranges. In the Nepal study, however, movements increased in the mating season.

The two panda species live in harmony among the shadowed bamboo thickets. There is extensive overlap between their home ranges, even the sacrosanct core areas. The main part of the Wolong study area was shared by two to four red pandas and six to seven giant pandas, one female red panda sharing as much as 70 per cent of her home range with five of the giant pandas. And for most of the year both species feed on the same species of bamboo in the same area. Yet there is little or no competition for food. This is because red pandas specialise in eating young bamboo leaves while giant pandas eat mainly stems and older leaves for most of the year.

The red panda depends as much as the giant panda on scent for communicating identity, intent, reproductive status and mood. Both males and females have paired anal glands (unlike the glandular patch of skin in the giant panda) that open on an area of bare, indented skin around the anus. The glands release a pungent, oily fluid which is rubbed onto marking sites that are also visually prominent. Going a stage further in the perfume stakes, red panda have also evolved supplementary transmission and detection equipment. Glandular pores on the soles of their feet produce a clear, colourless fluid, and long, coarse hairs around the pores brush this palm scent onto the ground, and leave a paper chase of messages. A cluster of elongated papillae on the tip of a red panda's tongue allow it to detect scent messages, tasting rather than smelling them. This facility is particularly useful on cold days when the chemicals in scents become less volatile and difficult to detect by sniffing. On these occasions, a red panda will inspect a scent-post by touching the area with the undersurface of its tongue.

Red panda males excel themselves when it comes to scent-marking. They do not just urinate or deposit scent like their larger relative, they do both. According to Schaller and his team, a male:

'straddles a small stump or other protuberance, squats, squirts urine several times with lateral movements of his rump, then deposits scent with circular rubbing motions. On occasion, a male legcocks, resting a hind paw on a vertical surface, while he marks.'

Females are more circumspect in their marking habits; they leave urine signalling to the males and deposit only scent.

Red panda latrines tend to be concentrated in favourite food patches. The numerous feeding trails radiating from the latrine area, suggest that an animal will remain localised for days at a time, exploiting patches of juicy-leafed bamboo. Red panda males are like their giant panda counterparts in scent-marking more than females[49] but, in Wolong, their marking does not vary from season to season as it does for giant pandas. There are no obvious peaks of frantic marking activity, even in the mating season, probably because males do not have to compete for females; they already 'own' females by virtue of defending a territory that contains two or three of them. Most scent-posts seem to double as resting sites, places the size of a doormat where the ground is tamped down and where piles of droppings line their perimeter. Accepted belief has it that red pandas rest mainly in trees and they do indeed do this in Langtang National Park in Nepal during the summer and the monsoon season, lying in firs at heights of 10 m (30 ft). But in Wolong red pandas rest at ground level or within a metre or two of the ground. The sites are a mixture of styles and textures – the top of fallen logs or next to them, inside tree stumps, verandah-style among the root systems of trees, and in the open, rocky outcrops, the top of large tufts of dead grass and excavated hollows in the snow and earth. None of them is specially constructed. Like their larger relative, red pandas plump for ready-made *chaises longues*. During one of his forays into the bamboo forest at Wolong, television assistant cameraman, Chris Catton, came across a red panda lying on its side, completely at ease: 'On our approach, it slowly raised its head and looked towards us. When we were within 60–80 m (196–262 ft) of it, the red panda rose sluggishly as if stiff and then disappeared into the bamboo. It always appeared alert and yet its locomotion was phlegmatic.'[50]

Vocalisations begin where scent-marking ends. Red pandas share about seven of the giant panda's calls and further studies might reveal more similarities.[51] Huffs, snorts, chomps, bleats (more like twitters in the red panda), chirps, squeals and barks all have the same sound and function in both species. But the honks, growls, moans and roars of the giant panda are absent in red panda language. And neither species has the loud keckering call of nursing bear cubs which is used to stimulate milk production in the mother. But two calls that the red panda has and the giant panda does not are the quack-snort, which indicates surprise, and the wha, a loud, often repetitive contact call. To the local peasants, the wha call sounds like the cry of a child and they know the red panda as the 'child of the mountain'.

Red panda faces are mobile and expressive. This means that a red panda can convey detailed information on mood and intention during close-contact encounters. The varied facial markings of red pandas also allow for individual identification. Apart from mother-infant associations, friendly meetings most often occur in the prelude to mating. In aggressive encounters, as between two territory-owning males, the opponents signal first-stage antagonism in a quite different way from the giant panda. They sometimes head bob like their giant relative[52] but raise rather than lower their heads, cocking their ears and arching their backs and tails. If one of the opponents backs down, he shows this by holding his head low and flattening his ears back against his head, a submissive posture shared by the giant panda. If neither animal backs down, then the second-level threat posture is engaged and the two animals stand up on their hind legs and hiss. If it escalates into a full-blown fight, the animals will follow the form of the giant panda, lunging and swiping at each other with their forepaws and attempting to bite each other on the back and rump. A fighting pair of red pandas will also rise up and hold the forepaws above the head before lunging.

While red pandas are long on close-contact sign language, they are short on the 'written' word. Only ground pawing and rolling and rubbing find a place in a red panda's visual communication system. Bark stripping, tree biting and tree clawing are not part of the repertoire.

Studies on animals in captivity provide the only information on longevity and the age of sexual maturity. Under such artificial conditions, red pandas reach sexual maturity between the ages of 18 and 20 months and live for as long as 14 years, although 10 or 11 is more usual. Little, too, is known about other aspects of red panda population dynamics as no sizeable wild groups have been studied.

There is, therefore, no information on any population as to the proportion of the different age classes, the survival rates in each class, or birth and death rates. The Nepal study did, however, find a dangerously high mortality rate in cubs due to human activity in the area, an alarming finding, given the precarious nature of red panda breeding behaviour.

CHAPTER 7

RAISING A FAMILY

Giant pandas are slow breeders. They are not unusual in this as all large mammals, particularly carnivores, are slow breeders, with a reproductive profile that designates them as being 'K-selected' species as opposed to being 'r-selected'. The main differences between the two groups are size of animal, population density and the time-frame of birth, life and death. R-selected species are relatively small and for them life is short but productive. Everything is speeded up and there is more of everything: more young per litter; more litters per female per year; the young are reared more quickly; offspring mortality is high; the age of sexual maturity is measured in weeks rather than years; and both reproductive life-span and actual life-span are short. Population density and its absolute size are great but there are often sharp swings in numbers – cycles of population explosions and crashes that are linked to food supply and predator numbers. As far as mammals are concerned, rats, rabbits and voles are examples of extreme r-strategists. Such species can usually easily weather the storms of a rapidly changing environment, both short-term and long-term, as the quick population turnover aids recovery of numbers and genetic adaptation.

K-selected species are relatively big and approach life at a more sedate pace. They produce a litter, at most, every year or two and the number of young per litter is limited to about one to three, but their survival rate is higher. The young are dependent on their mother (or both parents) for a relatively long period and sexual maturity is reached after several years. Population densities are close to maximum and do not swing between highs and lows, and while life-spans are longer, this does not compensate for the slower turnover. Consequently, population numbers are measured in thousands or tens of thousands rather than the millions or billions of most r-selected species. Elephants, lions, otters and giant pandas are all examples of K-selected species.

In giant panda society, members of the opposite sex must be compatible in order to commit themselves to mating. Putting a male and female together in an enclosure during the female's receptive period does not automatically make for a successful liaison. Too often, the male will either be aggressive or indifferent to the female's solicitations and so the relationship never gets off the ground. There is no chemistry and no copulation. In order to hit it off, would-be partners have to go through a series of lengthy olfactory and vocal exchanges. Only when they have both passed these tests will the pair engage in the close-contact interaction of courtship, and even then there can be a change of heart at the last minute on the part of the female if she has been courting more than one male.

Giant panda liaisons are the ultimate in short-lived passions. Females come into heat only once a year for about twelve to twenty-five days, with a critical peak of about two to seven days. It is in this short peak of oestrus that a pair must mate if it is to do it at all. The mating game starts around mid-March, when the snows still whiten the ridges and ravines of panda country, and continues to about mid-May, with a peak in April and early May. In the Qinling, Liang, and Min Mountains, some females also come into oestrus in autumn and winter, judging from various observations, such as the sightings of three adults together; trampled areas, where males presumably fought over a mate; and the estimated birthdays of young pandas that were identified in the area.[53] Perhaps, as Devra Kleiman of the Smithsonian Institution in Washington suggests, winter conceptions 'represent the vestige of a longer [mating] season in those animals that

*During the courtship phase of mating the partners
sometimes indulge in play*

once inhabited a more equitable climate at low altitudes'.[54] In captivity, females that fail to conceive in spring may show signs of a weak heat in September or October, but coupling occurs in spring; births in captivity are normally in late August and the first half of September.

Male and female giant pandas undergo noticeable behavioural changes during this period of peak heat. From being shy animals that shun direct contact they become sociable creatures earnestly seeking out other members of their species. They also become noisy. No longer the silence of pandas engrossed in the task of bamboo consumption and little else; now the green bamboo world resounds to the barks, roars, bleats and chirps of courting excitement. Schaller and his group heard wild pandas on thirty-two occasions and 87.5 per cent of these fell between March and May. Almost half of these were emitted during meetings of two animals and are likely to have been the sounds of courtship. There are also definite physiological changes. The testes of males enlarge and the level of androgens in their urine rises in the presence of females. Males also become much more active and scent-mark more frequently and vigorously, seeking out the females whose home ranges overlap with theirs. One to two weeks before peak receptivity, females lose their appetite and become more restless, bleating often and chirping once in a while as their thoughts turn to mating. A female will scent-mark more frequently and, as her vulva swells and reddens, she will rub it against objects or with her paw. Urine levels of oestrone, a by-product of oestrogen, increase as these changes occur and reach a maximum during the two- to three-day period of peak receptivity.

Males and females do not come face to face as soon as the females become receptive. They first of all have to sound out each other's suitability which they do by calling and by reading each other's scent messages. Once the male discovers that the female is about to reach her peak of receptivity, he will spend a few days following her around her home range, renewing old acquaintances or, if the resident individual has been replaced by someone new, forging a new relationship. This pre-courtship period allows both individuals to build a sound relationship and to coordinate their activities and test each other for compatibility. Without it, mating would not occur.

The extensive overlap between neighbouring male ranges is a sure recipe for competition among the tenants for the females that share common parts of their ranges. The calls of a courting couple or of a lone male advertising his presence may attract one or more other males to the area and lead to a competitive confrontation. During most of those encounters that the Schaller team was lucky enough to observe in Wolong, the males were of noticeably different sizes and the situation did not develop beyond a squabble as the smaller males gave way to the bigger ones. The team's field notes of 14 April 1983, a day of fog and heavy rain, describe a set-to between four males for the favours of a single female:

'A female sits in a fir about 10 m (30 ft) above ground. Wei (an adult male) bleats near the base of the tree. He climbs 3 m (10 ft) up the tree, but five minutes later descends and, in walking away, passes the observers at 2 m (6.5 ft). Another male, large and uncollared and with blood on forehead and ear, approaches then chases Wei a short distance. Wei, however, returns and once more climbs the tree in which the female sits; he bleats, she moans. Two minutes later Wei descends. An uncollared male is now near the tree too, as is the male Pi. The latter two face each other, moan, roar, and tussle until the uncollared male withdraws. At 0945, Pi ascends the fir and mounts the female, she crouched, bridging two branches, he balanced by her rump. Wei and the other male moan below. At 0956, Pi mounts the female for a minute and then once more briefly; at 0959, he places a forepaw on her back, sniffs her anal area and mounts as she chirps. Meanwhile yet another male has appeared, and the three squabble around the base of the tree.'

Pi and the female then climbed down and remained among the three males for a short while. Surprisingly perhaps, there was no fracas between Pi and the males but this was probably because, being easily the biggest and most assertive, Pi had highest rank and had established his right to the female. Later that same day, however, Pi fought fiercely

Male attempting to mate with female in the Wolong Giant Panda Reserve

with a large male more his size. Through roaring, growling and swatting, they tried to bite each other with wide open mouths and Pi eventually did bite his opponent's shoulder and chased him over a 6 m (19 ft) high precipice.

This courtship session went on for two to three days, but another lasted for less than half a day. During mating, which occurs at intervals during courtship, a female stands on all fours and indicates her submission to the male by crouching and presenting her rump. She lowers her head, sometimes tucking it right under so that her forehead rests on the ground or tree branch. Zhen, a wild female in Wolong, crouched in this way and then, in a further indication of submission, covered her eyes with her forepaws. Normally, the male approaches from behind and sniffs the female's anal area, and then, standing or squatting, he props himself up by resting his forepaws on her back and mounts. The female may remain crouching for minutes on end during which time the male dismounts and mounts frequently, but briefly, sometimes thrusting. Frequent mountings are a feature of species with induced ovulation, such as cats and rabbits – that is, they need the stimulation of repeated copulations in order to ovulate. In these animals there is lag period of one to two days between mating and ovulation and the male remains with the female for this period to prevent other males from getting to her at the crucial point of egg release. Giant panda males do not do this, despite their frequent mountings, which suggests that females are spontaneous ovulators. Their eggs are released in response to their own internal clock which interacts with the external rhythms of the environment.

It is not unusual for females to allow other males to mate with them. The same female that Pi mated was later that day seen mating with another smaller male. Even more noteworthy was the fact that the next day another medium-sized male mounted her in the presence of Pi. Pi was obviously confident that he had mated the female at exactly the right time – as she was about to ovulate – rather than too soon or too late. According to Schaller *et al*, his sperm must somehow achieve priority over other sperm that may have been deposited before or after ovulation. This suggested that Pi was either better than the other males at detecting the precise point of ovulation or the other males were equally adept but could not do anything about it, being of lower status. Whichever was the case, it seems that most adult males get the opportunity to mate during any one mating season but they will not necessarily all father offspring.

Female pandas call the mating tune. Copulation revolves around their period of peak heat but once this has ended all moves to mate stop until the next season. The giant panda's fleeting sociability ends and it resumes its solitary existence.

It is impossible to predict when a giant panda will give birth even when the date of conception is known. This may sound strange but it is because giant panda gestation is very variable, from three to five and a half months. And this, in turn, is because of 'delayed implantation' of the embryo, an adaptation found in a number of other temperate species such as roe deer and bears. The fertilised egg develops to the blastocyst stage, a ball of cells no bigger than a pin-head, but then, instead of implanting in the womb as it does in most mammals, it remains free-floating. Only when an increased production of progesterone is triggered does the womb thicken and the blastocyst implant.

During the Pleistocene, when pandas extended over 16 degrees of latitude, such opportunism may have been important to panda survival. Species that are able to 'predict' in advance when optimal conditions will occur so that implantation can take place at the appropriate time are at an advantage over those that cannot.[55] The sort of external cues that pandas may use to predict favourable conditions in a stable environment are day length, temperature and rainfall, although the latter is less reliable. Secondary, less accurate, cues include fluctuations in the availability of nesting sites, ground cover and the abundance of predators. If conditions are favourable, the blastocyst will implant but if food is scarce and the female's nutrition is below par, then the blastocyst will continue to float free in the womb. This explanation certainly fits with the fact that the period of delayed implantation in giant and red pandas occurs during the lean season when, both in terms of quality and calories, panda food falls below par. One must assume that if food conditions were to remain poor, the blastocyst would not implant and the female would be saved from the energy drain of pregnancy. Judging from the very undeveloped state of a newborn giant panda, development from the blastocyst stage to birth probably only takes about six weeks which means, given the gestation period, that the delay in implantation varies from about one and a half to four months.

Pregnant giant pandas are bound by the ageless imperative of nest building. They seek out suitable den sites – caves, dense bamboo thickets or hollows at the bases of trees – and line them with any material that will keep out the damp and cold and provide a comfortable cushion. Wood chips, birch and fir saplings, and branches of rhododendron or bamboo provide the necessary materials. Because dens have to be roomy enough for the female to sit upright comfortably, a tree must be at least 90–100 cm (35–39 ins) in diameter at breast height and have a large hollow. Such trees are at least 200 years old and are uncommon, especially in young or logged forests. The scarcity of these premier den sites may, in some areas, actually be more of a limiting factor on giant panda survival than the quality and supply of bamboo.

Information on panda birth and development comes largely from studies of captive animals, but observations on two wild females in Wolong, Zhen and Han, and an unnamed female near Fengtongzhai Reserve, have helped to put these data into perspective. Once the nest has been prepared a few days before birth, the female loses interest in food and water. Her nipples and vulva become swollen and she squats or sits to give birth. Giant panda labour should be among the easiest of all mammals if the tiny size of the infant, relative to its mother's size, is anything to go by. When the head of the young appears, she may help the rest of the infant to emerge by gripping it between her jaws and pulling gently. The infant is usually nursed immediately, the female pressing it against her breast with a forepaw, but Washington Zoo's Ling-Ling suffered a rather more shocking entry into the world. The rat-sized cub emerged with surprising force and shot across his mother's abdomen, landing on the concrete floor of the cage. He lay

*Giant panda mothers rarely allow their infants out of arms' reach.
Even at three months, the female feels secure only when her infant is in
her arms*

unmoving for several minutes until Ling-Ling accidentally touched him with her paw and stimulated him to squawk loudly. This was enough to trigger a response in his seemingly indifferent mother. She picked him up and nursed him immediately.[56]

Newborn giant pandas are exceptionally small at birth, a mere one-nine hundredth of their mother's weight. Indeed, the giant panda holds the record among placental mammals for having the largest mother: newborn weight ratio. They are blind and toothless and pink and naked except for a sparse covering of white hair. But for all its fragility, indeed because of it, a newborn panda has a very loud voice totally out of proportion to its tiny body. Having a mother big enough to crush you with an accidental swish of her paw or a languid stretch of her body makes it essential to let her know quite unambiguously that you are feeling discomfort. Natural selection has long since weeded out the feeble criers. An infant's repertoire is limited to one call only, a loud squawk, which is simple but very effective and is all a baby panda needs. Panda cubs lack the high-pitched grunts and loud, harsh purrs (keckering) of nursing ringtails (a species of racoon) and bears, calls which are thought to stimulate their mother to release milk and to take up a suitable nursing posture.

An infant giant panda is often nowhere to be seen, tucked beneath the mother's chin or hidden under a large hairy forepaw as she reclines. Sometimes the only sign of a cub is a long pink tail, proportionately much longer than an adult's, sticking out from under the female's paw. The baby suckles frequently in the first few days of life, about six to a dozen times a day for up to thirty minutes each time. The mother seems aware that any rough handling on her part could spell the end of a young life even before it begins and so she compensates by being especially gentle, holding the baby in her jaws across its shoulders or back, or clasped against her body with her forepaws.

The den is a vital refuge for the mother and her young from birth to about one month. A female does not travel much in the early days of baby care but is very restless and shifts her position time and time again. The wild female, Zhen, remained within a 200 m (656 ft) radius of her den for a whole month, venturing out to forage and drink for short periods only, but a sharp increase in the number of times she changed from one activity to another (as monitored by her radio-collar) indicated that she had become very restless. During this fidgety period, the female is not very interested in food and does not defaecate or urinate very often. In fact, she is more concerned with making sure that the baby does all these things that she does not. Between bouts of suckling and vigorous grooming, she encourages the cub to urinate and defaecate by licking its anus and, like a great many mammalian mothers, she eats the baby's wastes. It is interesting that while pandas will tolerate piles of droppings on rest sites, these are not permitted inside dens. Mother pandas keep their dens clean, either leaning out of the den entrance to defaecate or moving further afield. Captive females are equally fussy and urinate and defaecate as far away from the nest as possible. Such attention to hygiene reduces the risk of infections in the cubs. In addition to an outside toilet, a handy source of drinking water is another important amenity for a lactating female confined to the nursery. In Wolong, all three breeding dens in use were positioned near rivulets.

By the end of the first week, the black of the eye patches, ears and shoulders is just visible, and by the middle of the following week, the black has extended into the adult pattern. The hair, too, is denser. The infant looks like a miniature adult by the third week of life, apart from its tail which is still long. The eyes are open fully around week seven and the infant can raise its head and crawl by this time, but its coordination is still poor. The end of the second month sees the baby suckling about half as frequently as it did at birth and this declines further with age. The first teeth, either canines or incisors, appear towards the end of the third month. The infant can now walk, albeit clumsily. At 5 months of age, the young panda is well in control of its movements, walking, trotting, rolling around playfully and climbing onto its mother's back.

When it comes to baby care the giant panda is without peer. Nursing is initially very intense, with the female being in almost constant body contact with her newborn for the first three weeks. She holds her baby close to her even when she pops out of the den to relieve herself. A female observed by loggers near Fengtongzhai did not, however, abide by this rule. Not only did she leave the cub unattended in the den for as long as two to three hours while she fed, but the young did not squawk in objection. Normally, though, it is only when it is a well-furred and robust 1 month old, weighing 1 kg, or just over 2 lbs, less likely to be injured, and no longer needing the warmth of its mother, that she lets it out of her sight. And this no longer meets with squalls of protest from the infant. The squawk becomes more tempered and gradually disappears. The female can now afford to be a little less careful when she grasps her young. Any appendage conveniently to hand, whether paw or neck, is grabbed and such rough manhandling meets with no resistance.

The female moves her infant permanently out of the den around this time (four to seven weeks after birth). She resumes her normal travel pattern around her home range as she can now carry baby around with her. She probably does so in her mouth or, on longer journeys, cradled in one arm or hugged to her chest with a forepaw, although villagers once saw a female struggling with a cub under her armpit! As soon as she has found a good patch of bamboo, she very probably hides it among the dense bamboo stalks while she feeds nearby. When the cub is able to walk at 5 months of age, it is no longer allowed to hitch a ride on its mother.

At 6 months of age, the cub has a set of 26 to 28 teeth (all except the molars) which it puts to good use in starting to eat young bamboo leaves. Some two to three months later, around spring of the following year, young pandas become adept at consuming and digesting bamboo shoots. Now fully weaned and nutritionally independent of their mothers, they are still not yet ready to leave the nest and establish home ranges of their own. For one thing, they are still vulnerable to large predators, and for another, they need more experience in social communication and interaction. So they remain with their mother all through the breeding season, during which her normal mating urges are suppressed, and throughout summer and autumn. The young pandas, now hulking $1\frac{1}{2}$-year-old sub-adults of

During their first year of life, the cubs are active and playful. Only gradually do they take on the more phlegmatic personality of the adult giant panda

almost adult weight, take their leave just before winter begins in earnest.

The red panda is rather less of a K-selected species. Among its K-selected characteristics are a single fixed breeding season, a high percentage of surviving young, small litter size and a relatively long gestation period. But in a number of ways, the red panda is closer to the r-selected behavioural profile. They raise their young more quickly than giant pandas, produce litters more frequently (about once a year), reach sexual maturity at a younger age and have a shorter life-span.

Unlike the spacing patterns in giant panda society, the territories of male red pandas do not overlap. They do, however, overlap with parts of several female territories and because of this, there is no congregation of males competing for the favours of females as in the giant panda. Males seek out the females within their own ranges and attempt to mate with them as soon as the females are receptive. The receptive period is January to February, earlier than the giant panda's but, like its giant relative, the peak lasts for just one to three days, so male overtures have to be timed precisely. It is during this crucial period that ovulation occurs. Egg release is also spontaneous in the red panda and does not need the stimulus of mating to trigger it.

No one has ever observed red pandas courting and mating in the wild, but studies of animals in captivity give us a good idea of what must go on. Miles Roberts and David Kessler observed male-female pairs at the National Zoological Park in Washington, DC.[57] During the red panda's mating season, from mid-January to February, males follow females at a distance and mirror their daily activities. Whenever the female marks – and she does so more frequently at this time – so, too, does the male; when she rests, he rests. In the twenty-four hours prior to mating, marking increases dramatically and the female becomes agitated, rubbing herself against objects and arching her tail stiffly as she moves around. The male, for his part, sniffs the female repeatedly in her anogenital region and both of them whistle and twitter, calls which inhibit aggressive and defensive inclinations. In the typical invitation posture, a female stands with her rump up in the air and her back arched, shoulders and head lowered to the ground, and tail held well down and at right angles to her body. This mating posture is known somewhat grandly in biology as lordosis. The male approaches from behind and mounts the female dorsally, clasping her about the abdomen with his forepaws but, unlike the giant panda, refraining from biting her. The male rests between copulations, continuing to clasp the female, and both engage in a great deal of mutual grooming. The mounting pattern in red pandas is different from that in its larger cousin. Mounts are few and far between but prolonged, lasting up to twenty-five minutes; in the giant panda they are frequent and brief, no longer than two and a half minutes. Another notable difference in mating patterns between the two species is in the number of copulations an individual makes in any one season: just one for captive red pandas, but certainly more than one for giant pandas.

Following in the tradition of the giant panda, the red panda male takes no further part in raising a family. His contribution to the next generation ends with the short mating period.

In spite of the big difference in body size between the two panda species, gestation lengths are very similar. Studies of red pandas in captivity report gestation lengths of between ninety and 145 days, the shortest occurring at the lowest latitudes and the longest at the highest latitudes. It is generally accepted that this is the result of delayed implantation.

The average gestation period of 131 days means that red pandas give birth in June and July, two or three months earlier than the giant panda's birth season. The fact that these two species, both living in the same area and both dependent on the same food, have different breeding cycles is a sure sign of different energy priorities. The shift forward in the red panda's cycle means that the young become nutritionally independent early enough (in September) for them to take advantage of the fact that bamboo leaves are still tender and high in protein at this time of year. It also means that they are fully weaned by the time winter sets in and so that they are no longer an energy drain on the female who would otherwise find it very difficult to provide enough milk on an inferior winter diet.

Once a red panda female selects her den – a rock cave or tree hollow – she lines it with leaves and tree branches, and is then ready for the trials of labour. The females in a population tend to give birth within one and a half to two and a half days of one another, a sign that some sort of synchronising mechanism is in operation. Births in captivity indicate an average litter size of 1.7 young, the same as for the giant panda although this is more variable (one to four compared with one to three). The Nepal field study revealed a lower average of 1.2, probably a more realistic figure for conditions in the wild. A cub is more likely to survive if it is born in a litter of one or two than in a litter of three or four. It also stands a better chance if its mother is not a first-time mother. Newborn red pandas are a uniform buff colour, but by $2\frac{1}{2}$ months of age, just prior to their emergence from the nest, they have acquired the adult pattern and colour. Among placental mammals, the cubs of red pandas and procyonids rate as heavy in relation to the mother's weight. By contrast, the giant panda is at the top of the league table of light cub weight, while bears lie somewhere in between.

Red panda cubs are not only relatively heavier at birth, they are also more developed. Blind and toothless they may be, but they do not need the intensive care that giant panda cubs are given. Not only are they born more developed and better furred, and so do not depend as much on the warmth of their mother, but their nests are less exposed to the weather and less vulnerable to the attacks of predators. It is only for the first ten days that red panda females stay close to their young; they leave them only for short periods to eat, drink and attend to bodily functions. A red panda mother follows the den etiquette of carnivores and eats her cub's faeces during early development, normally until the cub starts on solid food. The young depend totally on their mother's milk for the first three to four months and weight gain is rapid – similar to that of racoons – despite the female having a bamboo diet. This is probably because the female boosts the cub's calorie intake by mobilising her fat reserves. Weaning begins at $4\frac{1}{2}$–5 months and is complete by 6 months of age, the cub's teeth erupting in good time to cope with the bamboo food.

The ties between mother and cub gradually weaken over winter. The female becomes more intolerant of her charges and will try to avoid them, deterring further close contact with low intensity threat displays. The apron strings are finally cut as the next breeding season approaches, when the cubs are about 8 months old. But it takes another ten months before they themselves can set up territories and breed. Until then, they are the transients of red panda society, moving through the territories of resident adults and gathering the experience and confidence that will serve them well in later life.

CHAPTER 8

SURVIVAL
STATUS

We are all used to thinking of the giant panda as one of Nature's failures, a loser whose numbers have already fallen 'naturally' to such a low level that eventual extinction is inevitable, the final twist in a long downward spiral of the species' incompetence. Nothing could be further from the truth. The major quandary facing the giant panda today is not how to become better adapted to the natural world (it already is) but how to adapt to degradation of and encroachment on its living space by Man.

It was not always so. Fossil remains of pandas are scattered widely throughout China, attesting to their successful colonisation of this vast area. But the evolution of the giant panda is a mystery. The animal appears suddenly in fossil records about three million years ago (Early Pleistocene) with no clear-cut ancestors. The provenance of the red panda is a little less fuzzy. A very distant ancestor of the firefox is thought to have been *Sivanasua* sp., a racoon-like fossil from the Oligocene and Early Miocene (twenty-five to thirty million years ago). A much later red panda 'prototype', *Parailurus*, more closely resembled the red panda. Although this species was larger than the red panda, it is nevertheless considered to be the most likely progenitor of the present species. *Parailurus* fossils have been found in North America and Europe, unlike red panda fossils, which appear to be confined to Asia, as are the fossil remains of the giant panda.

There were, in fact, two giant panda species living during the Pleistocene: a mini-giant panda about half the size of the present-day *Ailuropoda melanoleuca* (Early Pleistocene) and a creature indistinguishable from the present-day giant panda whose fossilised remains date from the Mid-Pleistocene. Both species ranged widely over China, and fossils seem to be absent only from the Yellow River and Yangtze River lowlands, the so-called eastern plains of China. Their altitudinal limit appears to have been much lower than that of pandas today. It is, in fact, impossible to state the lower limit of the giant panda's range in those days. The lack of fossils in the Yangtze/Yellow River lowlands may have been due more to poor fossilisation in the alluvial plains than to an absence of pandas (see Appendix 4, Map 2).

Altogether, evidence of giant panda occupation has been found at forty-eight sites in fourteen provinces in China,[58] from Sichuan westwards almost to Shanghai, and from southern Yunnan to as far north as Beijing. Fossil remains have also been discovered in northern Vietnam as far south as Vinh and in one location in Burma. Almost all the sites date from the Pleistocene era, evidence of the species' far wider distribution during this epoch than is the case now. This may have been partly due to a climate that was more favourable to the giant panda. It was warmer and wetter in those days, and bamboo (and with it all the pandas) are thought to have expanded their range during such meteorological golden periods, and to have been forced to contract their range to mountain refuges when cooler and drier conditions prevailed, as they did during the Late Pleistocene and the Holocene Period (the age we are presently living in). But while some of the decrease in panda distribution may very well have been due to climatic changes, the population crash that occurred cannot be so easily blamed on 'natural causes'.

The evidence presented by Zhu and Long show that various Chinese classical texts reported the presence of giant panda from as far afield as Jiangxi Province on the south-eastern coast of China. Three years before its 'discovery' by Père Armand David the giant panda could still be found in Hubei Province. And as little as 180 years ago the animal was still seen in Hunan, more than 500 km (310 miles)

Leaf-feeding. The giant panda's specialised forelimb allows it to process the enormous quantities of bamboo it needs to survive

from its nearest present-day habitat. Today, it clings precariously to life in six tiny mountain areas, the Qinlingshan in Shaanxi Province, the Minshan which straddle Gansu and Sichuan Provinces, and the Qionglaishan, Liangshan, Da-Xiangling and Xiao-Xiangling ranges in Sichuan Province (see Appendix 4, Map 3).

Red panda distribution has also shrunk considerably especially in this century. It was once found in a wide band that extended from northern India (Kashmir and Assam) through Nepal, Sikkim, Bhutan, northern Burma, southern Tibet and into the Chinese provinces of Yunnan and Sichuan. Since the forties, however, it has disappeared from much of its Himalayan range. Though data are scarce, it is now acknowledged that the red panda is extinct from eastern Kashmir, Sikkim and Assam and that it can no longer be found over much of Nepal. Its status in northern Burma is precarious and the ongoing guerrilla war there, together with lack of protection, hold little promise of a secure future in that region. The Bhutan populations are probably among the safest at present, as much of the primary forest there still remains intact. The picture in China is unclear, but it seems certain that the red panda is afforded a degree of protection wherever its range overlaps with that of its larger relative in the giant panda reserves. Along with most other rare species, it is also protected by numerous laws enacted over the past forty years.

After Liberation, in 1949, the government of the People's Republic of China were quick to recognise the unique status of the giant panda. It was designated a National Treasure and, in tandem with several other species, accorded protection by the Chinese Constitution: Article 9 of the constitution states that 'the government will protect rare flora and fauna'. Such blanket, though rather vague, protection was extended under the Forestry Law of the People's Republic of China, enacted in September 1984, in which cutting of forests (Articles 19 and 27), grazing of domestic livestock (Article 19) and illegal hunting (Article 21) are all forbidden. At the time of writing, the giant panda and its smaller cousin are further protected by a number of laws pertaining to all rare and precious species. The Wild Animals Protection Act of March 1989 stipulates a prison sentence of not less than seven years and a fine, or both, for anyone caught hunting a nationally protected species. Any person found trading or smuggling a nationally protected species (or skin, or any part thereof) can be dealt with even more severely. Under amendments to the laws against speculation and smuggling, passed in 1987, anyone guilty of such an offence can expect a sentence of ten years or more. The amendment also states that 'in serious cases the offender can be sentenced to life imprisonment or death, with confiscation of all property'. It is a mark of the gravity with which the Chinese authorities view illicit trade in pandas that such extreme measures have recently been implemented in full against a number of offenders. Thirteen people have been sentenced to life imprisonment for smuggling skins and at least one person has been executed by firing squad.

Strong measures must certainly be taken to stamp out poaching. As far as the adult giant panda is concerned, the species has never, naturally, suffered from predation and it has therefore evolved no mechanism to cope with this threat to its existence. Hunting is a relatively new problem, stimulated in great part by demand for pelts from abroad, especially Japan, where a single skin can fetch upwards of US$200 000, about £110 000. This fact, together with the panda's low reproductive potential, means that even a sustained low level of hunting can have a disastrous, probably lethal, effect on the species' viability. This one threat alone is sufficient to push the panda over into the abyss of extinction.

Despite such severe penalties, poaching for pelts and other panda products continues. At least one part of the giant panda seems to be credited with aphrodisiac qualities. While in Wolong Giant Panda Reserve, we were told that a tourist had recently been approached outside one of the main hotels in Chengdu and offered two dried globular objects which the seller said were panda testicles, and 'very good for man problems'. The incident may well have happened. In 1991 a street seller in Chengdu, wearing the distinctive dress of a minority hill-tribe, asked us to buy the contents of her sack. This turned out to be the foreleg and paw of a fully grown tiger. We asked the woman to wait, intending to return with personnel from the

Forestry Department, but she took fright and melted away into the crowd with the tiger limb clutched firmly in her hand.

Poaching may not even be intended to harm the pandas. Hunting is often carried out with the help of dogs and the disturbance produced in any hunting foray may be enough to stress the pandas and cause them to leave the area. Many pandas are also killed accidentally; they fall foul of snares set for other animals, especially the musk deer. The male of this small secretive deer produces a thick oily secretion, musk, from a gland or 'pod' located in its groin. Musk is highly regarded in Chinese medicine, and in the West as a base for perfumes. As a result, it is much in demand, and the price is high. The capture of one of these deer is the Chinese farmer's equivalent of winning the pools. With an average yearly income of around eight hundred Yuan (around ninety pounds) the four hundred Yuan that a single musk deer pod can command will radically alter a farming family's finances for the next twelve months. Small wonder, then, that the practice is hard to eliminate, even within giant panda reserves. In Wolong Reserve at least two giant panda have been killed by snares since research began in earnest during the late seventies, one of them a radio-collared animal who was very important to the ongoing studies being carried out into panda behaviour.

Harsh penalties against logging have also failed to prevent timber logging and agriculture from cutting deeply into the giant and red pandas' habitat. Deforestation of panda habitat is unequivocally the greatest threat facing both species. China suffers from a serious timber shortage and logging is an essential activity to provide wood for the construction industry. Logging teams from the provincial forestry departments are charged with extracting timber from natural forests, and with replanting. Surprisingly, forestry need not be incompatible with panda conservation, but it must be carried out sympathetically so as to keep disturbance to a minimum and to allow the forest to regenerate within a reasonable time with a natural balance of plant species, including bamboo. Unfortunately, many logging teams resort to clear-felling of trees. This practice seriously affects the ability of the area to sustain pandas. John MacKinnon, who has spent many months studying giant panda distribution, believes that the activities of timber units can explain many of the apparent gaps in giant panda distribution. And, apart from the obvious effect of denying the panda cover, evidence is accumulating to show that clear-felling upsets the state of peaceful coexistence which has evolved between the bamboo and the trees. Though not obvious (many other factors, such as clear-felling and natural tree death, often confuse the picture), research now indicates that in any given area with a dense bamboo understorey, most of the trees are of the same age. When the date of germination of these trees is calculated, it turns out that it corresponds to the date of the last bamboo mass flowering. After the bamboo has seeded and died, the amount of shade beneath the bamboo culms decreases greatly. Tree seeds which would normally perish because of lack of light under bamboo stands now grow strongly. In effect, by dying back, the bamboo 'allows' the forest trees to re-establish themselves.

The trees seem to reciprocate this kindness. If bamboos germinate under the shade of the forest trees (around 30 per cent tree canopy cover is regarded as a minimum) the plants grow strong and vigorous. By contrast, most bamboo seed that germinates in a clear-felled area dies because of the excessive amounts of heat and light reaching the ground. Those bamboo seedlings that do survive never attain the height and vigour of their canopy-reared fellows. Because of this, panda conservationists are now urging that clear-felling be banned, that selective logging should spare at least some of the larger conifer species that are used for breeding dens, and that a canopy cover of at least 30 to 40 per cent should remain after logging to permit natural regeneration of both trees and bamboo. Only tree species native to the area should be replanted; at present, many logging teams replant an area with seedlings that are different from the original tree species, and the young trees are also planted so closely together that they prevent the growth of a bamboo understorey.[59]

Systematic, large-scale logging also produces damaging spin-offs in the form of the road and rail links necessary for the highly mechanised timber units to gain access to the forest and to transport the cut logs to market. Roads allow not only the logger to enter woodland more easily – poachers, too, are quick to take advantage of the opening up of previously inaccessible areas. Farmers also use the roads to make new incursions into the forest, clearing the land and tilling their fields at an increasingly higher altitude.

Peasant farmers are also responsible for a more insidious form of deforestation – wood-cutting for firewood and other domestic uses. Because such losses in forest cover occur piecemeal over many years, it is very difficult for managers of the giant panda reserves to form an accurate picture of the extent of the problem. Robert de Wulf and his co-workers have overcome this difficulty by using remote-sensing.[60] The earth has been photographed from orbiting satellites for more than two decades. The images can be used to extract various categories of information, including the extent of different vegetation types. For this particular study it was especially important to distinguish between forest and heavily disturbed woodland. LANDSAT satellite images of the giant panda areas between 1975 and 1983 were minutely examined by de Wulf and his colleagues, and the area of forest cover at the beginning and the end of this period was calculated. The results were dramatic and depressing. The photographs revealed that almost half of all panda habitat had been heavily disturbed or cut since 1975. Some of this degradation can be laid at the door of the logging units, but the major loss of forest is attributable to individual farmers taking relatively tiny amounts of wood for their own use. The wood is mainly used for heating during the long cold winter that affects the mountain valleys between November and March, but the cumulative effect of such cutting is worrying. While filming in Wolong, time and again we passed the villages of Qiang tribes-people where each house had an enormous stack of lumber outside the front door, often with a second wood pile drying off behind the house. With the easy availability of electricity (there are two dams in the Wolong Reserve that produce hydroelectricity), it is odd that the Qiang do not change from wood to electric current to heat their houses. We asked about this but were told by one official that the Qiang have cut wood in this manner since time immemorial, and 'old habits die hard'.

More alarming still is the pattern of such deforestation. When cutting wood, farmers and loggers quite naturally nibble away at the most accessible forest margins first. They also tend to keep to flat areas where the tree felling can be most easily effected. Regions such as passes between peaks are prime targets for the logger's axe and farmer's bill-hook. As a result, the forest comes more and more to resemble a filigree pattern, islands of panda habitat surrounded by agricultural fields. Roads and railways have also helped to isolate further the remaining woodland. And with such fragmentation of the habitat, panda populations have become increasingly isolated from one another as the years have passed.

In biological systems there is a lower limit of population, the Minimum Viable Population (MVP), below which there is very little probability of a population surviving long-term. And, while it is true, as population geneticist Michael Soule has said, that 'there is no single value or "magic number" that has universal validity',[61] as a rule of thumb, it is generally accepted that most species require at least 500 individuals to ensure their long-term viability and avoid the sometimes disastrous effects of inbreeding and random genetic movement. In geneticist's terms inbreeding results in more individuals who are homozygous for recessive deleterious genes, which basically means that hidden harmful characteristics show up more frequently in inbred populations, resulting in a loss of vigour, fertility, or both. There is also evidence that inbreeding can have a harmful effect on both the size of the litter and the survival of the young after birth.

Genetic drift is believed to occur in all isolated populations and is the natural consequence of sexual reproduction and the random mixing of genes. The frequency of genes that have no crucial survival value (i.e. are neither especially harmful nor especially beneficial) in any given environment tends to fluctuate randomly over the generations. Where the population is large, such genes normally manage to find a home in at least a few individuals. If in one generation a gene Y is randomly assigned to, say, only 1 per cent of a population numbering 1000 animals, it will be present in ten individuals of that generation. But if the total population numbers only 100, just a single animal will have gene Y. In a very small population of ten animals the gene will

Qiang tribespeople resting on top of a woodpile cut from panda habitat

appear in 0.1 animals – in other words, there is a 10:1 chance that gene *Y* will be lost forever from that group. This loss of genetic material may not prove immediately harmful, but it may limit the ability to cope with future environmental changes.

With the giant panda's population standing at around 1000 and a MVP 'lower limit' of 500, the species appears, at first sight, to be well within the MVP safety limits. Sadly, this optimistic assessment ignores new information on the degree of fragmentation of panda populations. The giant panda is already divided into six major population groups, none of which has sufficient numbers to reach the 'safe' MVP of 500. And worse, a recent panda survey has shown that the giant panda now exists in twenty-four separate populations, with very little chance of physically communicating (and therefore breeding) with one another. John MacKinnon and his co-workers on the survey estimated that 'most of these populations today number less than fifty individuals, and many as few as ten or less. Even within reserves, the populations are often fragmented and cut off from each other'. This is indeed bad news: a second rule of thumb in population genetics is that even short-term survival requires populations of at least fifty individuals.

One example will stand to demonstrate the disaster facing the species. On the general map of panda distribution on page 204, the area designated as the Min mountains shows giant panda distribution as a large stippled area some 13 300 km² (5000 square miles) in extent, the largest single area of remaining panda habitat. Panda numbers in the Minshan are higher – between 210 and 280 animals – than in any other area. So, on paper, we have a large panda area, with the greatest number of living pandas. Even so, with less than 500 individuals in the entire population, the long-term viability of the Minshan pandas must remain in doubt. And a closer look at the distribution of forest and pandas reveals an even more depressing prognosis. The Minshan pandas are broken up into at least six separate groups. Some (like Wanglang and Huanglongsi Reserves) are tiny, numbering ten animals or less, with almost zero probability of even one animal crossing over the barriers between the different panda groups to 'outbreed'.

This picture is repeated in every major panda reserve (see Appendix 5). Given such miserably small numbers in each population island, the prospects are bleak indeed. On this basis, most giant panda populations can be written off right now – unless Man steps in to ensure genetic interchange between populations, perhaps in the form of translocation of pandas from one area to another. Without action to redress the balance, the small size of most panda groups already marks them for extinction.

It would be wonderful if we could simply call a halt to any further poaching or degradation of the pandas' habitat. But, even if we did, the panda would in all probability still be doomed. We have already gone too far, the pandas' continued existence on this planet is now dependent on our careful management of their fragmented populations. To have any chance of survival, both the giant and the red panda must learn to live with a human population that has severely affected the size and quality of their habitat. Equally, Man, the author of all the pandas' woes, must take responsibility for his actions and manage the panda populations to ensure their long-term viability. Thankfully, there is evidence that we are now beginning, at least, to think seriously about the problem.

CHAPTER 9

SAVING THE PANDA

Since the seventies, Chinese and subsequently Western scientists have invested tens of thousands of man-hours in an attempt to unravel the mysteries of the red and giant panda's lifestyle. To biologists, such studies have their own internal validity; the information adds to the store of human knowledge and is worth having just for itself. But all too often in the past, this obsession with knowledge has blinkered scientists to the fact that the animal or plant concerned is being destroyed even as they study it. For some, extinction has been a side issue, the overriding imperative was placing the animal or plant in the 'big picture', obtaining an overview of all behaviour, of which one particular species is but a small part. They might pay lip-service to conservation, but that was someone else's job. The attitude has been 'let's get as much information about this beast before it disappears', with more cash spent on studying the minutiae of the species than on preserving it.

Lying back while feeding helps to conserve precious energy

The logical result of such an attitude is the library-zoo, shelf upon shelf of volumes describing in great detail the appearance and habits of all species in a host of now extinct ecosystems. Intellectually satisfying, perhaps, but ultimately pointless, a pale shadow of the vibrant living splendour such works can, at best, only half describe.

Fortunately, with the giant panda, and to a lesser extent with its smaller relative, the knowledge obtained over the past fifteen to twenty years is not being wasted. Recently, under the aegis of the Ministry of Forestry of the People's Republic of China and the World Wide Fund for Nature (WWF) a group of Chinese and Western scientists was charged with overviewing the current state of knowledge of the giant panda, its behaviour, biology, captive-breeding status, etc, and coming up with a detailed management plan that would ensure its continued long-term survival. These scientists, John MacKinnon of the United Kingdom, and Bi Fengzhou, Qiu Mingjiang, Fan Chuandao, Wang Haibin, Yuan Shijun, Tian Anshun and Li Jiangguo from China, have since delivered a 157-page document, the *National Conservation Management Plan for the Giant Panda and its Habitat* (NCMP), which gives detailed recommendations for the conservation of the species and its environment.[62] It is a splendid work; it pulls no punches when describing the perilous state that giant panda populations have reached, but it also offers hope with a series of recommendations that, if implemented swiftly, could yet prevent the panda's extinction. In essence, the giant panda can be saved by preserving its habitat. And this, in turn, will help to conserve a host of species which share the panda's habitat, creatures such as the takin, the golden monkey and the red panda. We have drawn heavily on this work, the most up-to-date exposition of the options open to panda conservation, in writing this chapter.

CAPTIVE BREEDING

Records of giant pandas in captivity go back as far as the Western Han dynasty (206 BC–AD 24). It was customary for the emperors of the day to keep a few dozen rare species in the palace garden at Xian for their delectation and the giant panda was the most coveted. Even in those days it was considered rare, but a naturally rare and secretive creature, not the threatened animal we know today. Because it was difficult to catch and, to most Chinese, more fable than fact, to own a captive panda was a mark of status, and one that only emperors could have. Because of their cachet, giant pandas have been used as diplomatic currency for hundreds of years. One of the early Tang dynasty Emperors sent two live pandas to Japan as a gesture of friendship to cement trading ties, and in 1972, Chairman Mao Zedong presented the National Zoo in Washington, DC, with two young adults to mark Richard Nixon's visit to China.

While they were much sought after, captive giant pandas were considered expendable. When they died, they were simply replaced with wild stock. Breeding them was not considered as there was no need. There was no place for the burning issues that confront us today, and questions such as 'is it right to subject captive animals to physical and psychological stress?' and 'what is the value of captive breeding?' were simply not a part of social concerns. Private ornament, status and diplomatic well-being were the main reasons for keeping wild animals in captivity and, as such, it was a privilege confined to aristocrats. Public menageries were still very much part of the future.

Zoos were established only 200 years ago. The Jardin des Plantes in Paris was inaugurated in 1793 and London Zoo in 1828. The attraction of these menageries, and of others that followed, were the exotic species that were being discovered in the colonies. It was entertainment and education for the public and profit for the zoos that encouraged such collections.

The red panda was the first of the two panda species to be exhibited alive in the West. On 22 May 1869, the same year Père David discovered the giant panda, London Zoo acquired the western world's first live red panda. It was the sole survivor of a group of three animals collected earlier that year near Darjeeling in northern India and its entry into public life in London was a surprisingly low profile affair. There was no fanfare, no superlatives from the press. The celebrated debut of the giant panda on the public stage came very much later, in

1936, when Ruth Harkness brought Su Lin, a juvenile, over to the United States of America. Journalists and photographers swamped the dockside in San Francisco eager to record the event. The historic moment was acknowledged by no less a couple than the Roosevelts. Perhaps the red panda's low-key entry into English society was because Western zoos were still in their infancy in the 1800s and were not accessible to a wide public. The fifty odd years that followed saw many more zoos established in Europe and the United States and zoo-going was much more a part of ordinary people's lives. Whatever the reason, the public display of Su Lin triggered a demand for giant pandas from zoos all over the world, including those in China itself. In 1937, two pandas were put on display at Shanghai Zoo, no doubt more for the benefit of the foreigners there than the locals. Even without the novelty advantage that Su Lin had enjoyed, later giant panda emigrants still guaranteed enormous crowds – and cash – throughout the year. Red pandas also began to make a definite though still rather muted impression on the crowds. Between 1950 and 1969, some 250 red pandas found their way over to European zoos. Today, there are over 150 red pandas and some forty giant pandas in zoos and wildlife parks outside China.

During the fifties and sixties, zoos became interested in breeding species in captivity, in part for the challenge itself, but also because rare species like the giant panda had immense monetary value. Chi Chi apparently earned US$2000 (about £1000) a week during her tour of Europe in 1958. A big demand for something that is rare and difficult to catch translates into a sizeable price tag. Today, the price of hiring a live pair of giant pandas costs up to US$600 000 (about £350 000). On 9 September 1963, Beijing Zoo made the headlines as the first zoo to breed the giant panda in captivity. The tiny star was christened Ming-Ming, the repetition of her name indicating the affection which the Chinese felt for her.

With the conservation consciousness of the seventies came an interest in captive breeding as a way of helping to save a species from extinction. For one thing, captive breeding meant that zoo demand for species could be met by captive specimens as opposed to wild

*Mother with captive-bred juvenile in Chengdu Zoo in China, one of the
world's most successful captive-breeding centres*

stock. This was important because the attrition on wild populations was much greater than at first sight; for every animal that reached a zoo, many more died at the hunting stage and again during the journey to their destinations. For another, animals bred in captivity could be reintroduced to the wild in those places where their habitat was still intact. The seventies also heralded the application of an important technique used in breeding domestic animals – artificial insemination. China again pulled off the first success in this when, in 1978, the giant panda Yuan Jing was born at Beijing Zoo.

But even as these efforts were being applauded, there were voices that questioned the use of captive breeding as a conservation tool. Among the principal objections was that of public perception, the concern being that breeding programmes might lull the public into a false sense of security in which they might think the problem of conserving endangered species was well in hand. It was feared this attitude would, in turn, take the pressure off governments to do something about preserving wildlife *in situ*. There were also biological problems, one such being genetic viability. With a small population to breed from, there was the very real problem of inbreeding and the consequent deleterious effects on the animal's 'evolutionary fitness' – its ability to reproduce its genes and at the same time weather the long-term changes in its environment.

Both captive populations of red and giant pandas are relatively small so the problem of genetic viability is a serious one, even if we suppose complete agreement and freedom to exchange animals between collections all over the world. A recent assessment, however, claims that there is, in fact, enough genetic variation in the current *Red Panda Studbook* collection to develop a long-term preservation programme.[63] But this prediction makes some highly optimistic assumptions. First, that the present zoo population produces 250 surviving offspring within the next generation, which is four and a half years. Second, that a minimum population of 500 individuals is maintained and that, in each future generation, there will be at least 125 pairs each producing two young per generation. Failing such an upbeat scenario, it was suggested that genetic exchange between wild and zoo populations might be the answer in maintaining genetic variability in both.

Associated with genetic viability is the worry of demographic viability. What this means is the need to maintain an equal sex ratio and a workable mix of different age classes, which in turn requires balancing recruitment rates with death rates in each age class. It is a juggling act that Nature accomplishes with ease, but one which needs careful analysis and scientific application for Man to achieve, especially if he is dealing with a small population. As far as the red panda and giant panda are concerned, the nettle of maintaining demographically viable populations in captivity is only just being grasped.

Those against captive breeding were also against reintroducing animals to the wild that had been bred in captivity. They agreed that breeding in captivity had a place in reducing the pressures suffered by wild populations in supplying zoo exhibits. But reintroductions were not acceptable because the animal being bred was adapted for captive conditions and not for survival in the wild. In short, would a panda bred in captivity be able to cope in the wild? Would it know how to look for and deal with its wild food? Would it know how to find a mate? Would it have the same resistance to disease or indeed, even more likely, might it not introduce new diseases to which it was genetically resistant but to which its wild brethren were susceptible?

Like most heated issues, the arguments became polarised but most conservationists today take a more balanced view. While they accept many of the criticisms against breeding, they see them more as problems to be solved rather than as precluding breeding in captivity. There are few biologists who would wish to consider a future where a rare species is known only as a zoo exhibit, no matter how proper its upkeep or how 'natural' its enclosure. And most of us agree that there is no point in breeding for reintroduction if the animal's wilderness home vanishes under axe or agriculture. Most biologists and responsible curators want to see wild species being preserved in their natural habitats, not only for Man's sake but also because ethics dictate that other living forms have this right. Biologists and their ilk, however, do not dictate social and economic policy, they can only

influence it. It needs the full complement of politicians, economists, town planners and law makers to take decisions that are sympathetic to both wildlife and people. It is a complicated process and, increasingly, one that needs global coordination in order for it to work. Only in this context does a breeding programme have any worth.

How successful have efforts been at breeding pandas in captivity? Because the red panda is a little further along the r-K selection spectrum, one might reasonably assume that if any of the two species would multiply more easily in captivity, it would be the red panda. But despite advances in animal husbandry, the *Red Panda Studbook* shows an abysmal record of recruitment since it was first started in 1978.[64] In the eight years between 1978 and 1986, 217 births produced a mere ten additions to the captive population, 42 per cent of newborn cubs and juveniles having died before reaching 6 months of age, and a further 53 per cent in early adulthood. At a recent conference on red pandas in Rotterdam, biologists and zoo keepers looked critically at the statistics and came to some stark conclusions.

The biggest culprit of cub death is stress. Females are not being given enough privacy in which to raise their offspring and as a result, some mothers anxiously shift their young from one place to the next. This gives the mother little time to suckle them, and milk production might also be affected. Food is another factor. Most zoos and wildlife parks find it impossible to supply red pandas with enough fresh bamboo to sustain their total needs. Other foods, such as fruit and vegetables, supplement their diet. Captive red pandas are very partial to this artificial menu, but it seriously affects their health. Post mortem examinations reveal severe liver damage that explains ailments such as enteritis, pneumonia, gastric disorders and circulatory disturbances.

Fertility in the captive red panda population has increased over the years but there is still much room for improvement. For an animal

Above left: Named Blue Sky (Lan Tian) by H.R.H. Prince Philip,
this young cub was the first panda to be captive bred at Wolong Giant
Panda Research Station

Below left: Mother with a year-old cub. Few zoos have succeeded in
mastering the skills necessary for successful panda breeding

to be considered fit enough to be part of a breeding programme, it should be free of external and internal parasites. In many cases, captive red pandas are infested with high levels of both and this may depress fertility. Normal hygiene and good veterinary care are all that are needed to prevent this.[65] Fertility and, indeed, survival generally, are also affected by susceptibility to disease, and red pandas in captivity are particularly prone to infections. One speaker at the conference felt that this could be due to a naturally low level of resistance, high resistance in the wild being unnecessary if you are a fairly sparsely distributed animal.[66]

While the captive red panda population is not in immediate danger of extinction, its future is by no means certain. Births have increased but they have not outstripped mortality, prompting the comment that 'if wild-caught individuals had not been available, the red panda would have long since disappeared from our zoos'. Zoo populations are still being bolstered by wild specimens as China continues to make red pandas freely available to zoos in Europe and the United States, despite legal protection. This may boost efforts to breed pandas in captivity, but it is not something that should be allowed to continue given the parlous status of the red panda in the wild. It is an indication of the lower priority Chinese and Western authorities give the red panda over its more famous relative.

The giant panda breeding programme has steered an unsteady course through many disappointments and much global media coverage. There is no more public a courtship than a giant panda's. Every bleat, every disinterested yawn, the mildest of rebuffs, are all reported by a press and read by a public hungry for more.

The problems begin with the sexing of pandas. There is little noticeable difference in size between males and females, and while some zoo keepers claim to be able to identify them from head shape, body size and behaviour (females being more sociable and less aggressive), these are not reliable features. Of course, if males had obvious genitals then there would not be a problem, but they do not. There is no scrotum, the testes lying within the body, and although they enlarge during the mating season, the thick layer of fat that protects them obscures any bulge. The penis, too, is normally hidden and so is of no help whatever in sexing. Many a mistake has been made in guessing the sex of a panda. The famous Su Lin was thought to be a female but 'she' turned out to be a he and this was only discovered at the animal's autopsy. Many other false sexings have been made, but even when a pair were correctly labelled, pairings produced more failures than successes. Chi Chi, London Zoo's female, and her mate, An An, from Moscow, repeatedly raised, and dashed, hopes. More newspaper articles came out of that liaison than any possibility of offspring.

Only three zoos outside China have bred giant pandas: Mexico, Madrid and Tokyo. Washington DC Zoo produced a live cub but it died within hours of birth. Chinese zoos have had greater success in absolute numbers of births (over fifty, up to 1986, at seven zoos), but only thirty-one have survived thus far and, seen in relation to the captive population of eighty animals, it is not very good. Beijing Zoo is top of the league with about thirty births to date, with Chengdu running second with seven births. In the period between 1980 and 1985, however, only nineteen young out of fifty-one births in Chinese collections survived two months or more – an infant mortality of 63 per cent. Of the fifty-one births, fourteen were twins, and even if we discount the abandoned cubs as a natural event (females do not normally rear more than one cub), we still get an infant mortality of 49 per cent. This is almost one and a half times higher than the highest juvenile mortality in a survey of twenty-nine species bred in captivity. Infant mortality is lower in other countries, where management is better and all the females of breeding age have borne cubs, but at 40 per cent, the figure is still far too high.

Clearly, the infant death-toll must be reduced, but there is also a great deal that can be done to increase conception. At present, only 15 per cent of China's captive population is breeding – three known breeding males and ten females. One of the females, Li-Li, lives at the breeding centre in Wolong Nature Reserve. This was set up in 1980 and, in 1986, produced its first cub. Christened Lan Tian (Blue Sky) by Prince Philip, the cub died in 1990 despite the centre having excellent veterinary facilities.

Despite their laid-back attitude to life, giant pandas can migrate considerable distances during periods of bamboo die-back

Giant panda breeding statistics read somewhat better than those for the red panda, but they are still poor and, given present levels of care and skills, translate into a non-viable captive population. This is primarily because there has been no systematic approach to the endeavour. The NCMP wants to change all that. It puts forward hard-hitting proposals for breeding in captivity within China, prefacing them with the statement that the giant panda breeding programme should aim to become self-sufficient without the need for input from the wild and that it should produce enough surplus pandas for reintroduction to the wild.

Step one of the captive breeding plan is the production of a studbook. That there is none at present is surprising considering that the red panda has had one for the past thirteen years. The studbook should register the approximate age, sex, breeding condition, breeding record and population origin of each animal, and details should be obtained on each institution's breeding facilities, animal care, breeding failures and causes of any deaths. Using the studbook as a database, the NCMP proposes a national breeding programme administered by a committee based in Beijing:

> 'All captive pandas should come under the responsibility of this committee and individual facilities shall only be permitted to continue holding captive pandas if they agree in writing to comply with the committee's recommendations with respect to breeding and movement of captive pandas. The commercial sale or exploitation of giant pandas would be prohibited and ownership of the captive pandas would be in the name of the national programme and not the individual facility. The committee shall designate an agreed proportion of the bred pandas for reintroduction into the wild.'

One NCMP recommendation echoed the findings of earlier studies in that breeding success can be increased by 80 per cent if males and females are allowed to get to know each other before the start of the breeding season instead of suddenly springing an arranged marriage on the unsuspecting pair. As one biologist put it, 'Familiarity does not breed contempt in giant pandas; it makes for breeding.' Artificial insemination should only be used if there are suitable females but no available males. And to this end, research should continue on improving techniques for collecting, preserving, transporting and inserting semen as well as developing better techniques for monitoring oestrus and pregnancy through behaviour, hormone tests, vaginal smears, etc.

Mothers about to give birth should be isolated and disturbed as little as possible, and after birth, they should be watched carefully for the first few days for signs of rejecting their babies or failing to feed them. If this happens, the cubs should be removed and hand-reared immediately, as should the smallest or weakest of twins, because females do not normally rear two offspring. Finally, any captive pandas that are sent overseas for exhibition should be immature animals or animals past breeding age (unless they are for a specific breeding loan) so as not to interfere with China's national breeding programme.

The authors of the NCMP feel that the main justification for keeping giant pandas in captivity today should be to restock wild populations – to help them recover from bamboo die-back, to speed up recolonisation of formerly occupied or replanted areas and to boost genetic diversity. To date, there have been few successful releases of pandas caught in the wild back into their natural habitat but no attempt to reintroduce pandas raised in captivity. Panda experts do not feel there should be any real problem with this as giant pandas in captivity instinctively know how to deal with bamboo. They do not need to be taught. What they need to learn is where to find bamboo in different seasons according to local conditions. This they learn in the wild from their mothers during the twelve months they remain with her after weaning. So it would make sense to release young adults (old enough to be immune to predators and aggressive resident pandas) with human guides or with wild-caught, experienced, adult foster mothers. This is already common policy in the rehabilitation of primates and other carnivores. Some attempts to reintroduce wild-caught giant pandas to the wild have failed because the animals were released into unfamiliar habitat which required experience in different seasonal ranging patterns and food selection. The patterns the panda remembers have no relevance in the new habitat and yet the animal automatically moves to this recorded tune. Its behaviour is not malleable enough to respond to immediate imperatives and if it is not recaptured, it dies.

With these general do's and don'ts in mind, the NCMP proposes four specific experiments:

1. The release of two-year-old captive born pandas in the Shiqiaohe Valley of Tangjiahe reserve. This valley has few wild pandas but plenty of *Fargesia* sp. bamboo with a simple enough distribution to make its exploitation straightforward without the need of a foster mother. The pandas are to be fitted with radio-collars to keep track of their movements and to assist recapture if this is deemed necessary.

2. Try fostering an 8–10-month-old infant onto a particular captive female (known to be a non-breeder) in a large outdoor enclosure at Wolong Breeding Centre. If the adoption is successful, foster mother and cub should be released together and the infant fitted with an expandable or 'breakaway' radio-collar (one designed to break off when the animal grows and the collar becomes too tight). Close monitoring of both animals will be essential so that if the infant is abandoned it can be rescued.

3. Use the existing holding pens and enclosure at Wanglang station in Wanglang Reserve for release trials. Young pandas will be transferred from the cages to the enclosure and, after fitting them with breakaway radio-collars, staff will then escort them on a number of trips into the surrounding bamboo forest. Once they have learned the necessary skills they will be allowed to roam freely and establish their own home ranges. Hunting is to be prohibited in this area and

Mountain forest – panda habitat or fair game for the logging units?

if any natural predators appear (e.g. leopards or hunting dogs), they should be captured and released far from the experimental area.

4. Build a holding pen in Foping Nature Reserve to hold sick or injured pandas rescued from the wild. Pandas that prove suitable for breeding should be kept for that purpose. Release trials, similar to those at Wanglang station, should be made at Zhenglongchang near Sanguanmiao guardpost. It is hoped that wild or released adult females may adopt them. Special attention should again be paid to natural predators and if these prove a problem, the young pandas should be recaptured and released in a safer area.

Many biologists believe that the future will see nature reserves and zoos becoming more and more similar. Nature reserves will shrink in the face of human pressures and zoos will become larger and more naturalistic in response to modern animal management. This is a depressing picture for some, but it may none the less be realistic. And as conditions in these two types of enclave become more similar so, too, will the problems and techniques of managing small populations of species.

RESERVE MANAGEMENT

Given the pivotal role of Mankind in determining the giant panda's ultimate fate, the primary directive in the panda reserves is the suppression of all human activities harmful to the species and its habitat. The NCMP is clear on this point. Within the giant panda reserves steps should be taken to prevent illegal grazing and hunting. Timber cutting, whether for the logging industry or local consumption, should be banned outright. Reforestation should take place where necessary (with care taken to re-establish a natural mix of native species), and bamboo understorey should be planted wherever there seems a likelihood that it will flourish. The practice of planting exotic bamboo species is not advised. In the past, exotic bamboos were thought of as a means of staggering bamboo flowering episodes, so that if the native bamboo flowered, there would still be the exotic species for the panda to feed on. There were even attempts to delay or stimulate bamboo flowering by spraying the plants with a number of chemicals (indole-acetic acid, gibberellic acid and nitrogen fertiliser). With our increased knowledge of the giant panda and the ecosystem it inhabits has come the realisation that such tampering would almost certainly prove counterproductive. The native bamboo species have evolved together in a particular habitat over many thousands if not millions of years, their presence influencing other plants and wildlife, including both the giant and the red pandas. Because they feed in a relatively small area and rarely move any further afield, for most of the time giant pandas naturally form small, inbred units. Bamboo die-back may actually aid the giant panda by forcing an otherwise home-loving animal (who would meet and breed with only a few neighbouring animals if die-back did not occur) periodically to move long distances in search of food and inadvertently to encounter new blood-lines.

It would quite clearly be folly to tamper with such a system, especially as, in the case of bamboo flowering, we are dealing with extended time scales – any disastrous consequences of artificial interference may not become apparent for thirty years or more.

Beyond the panda reserves the problems are even more pressing. More than half the total population of giant panda live in these areas, with minimal protection from the whole gamut of potentially fatal human activity. The management plan calls for the formal recognition of these areas as panda habitat, with steps being taken to reduce damage to these areas by strictly enforcing the bans against poaching, hunting and farming. Forestry procedures must also be regulated: no new logging units should be formed in panda habitat; cutting areas must be gradually reduced and clear-felling phased out in favour of selective logging, using small-scale operations and making sure that at least 30 per cent of the tree canopy is left intact.

If such recommendations are implemented, there should be no further attrition on either the pandas or their habitat. But this is only half the battle. As we have already seen in Chapter 8, the existing panda populations are already so small and so isolated that most, if not all, are likely candidates for extinction. The most far-reaching

The Qiang people of Wolong
Valley are of Tibetan stock.
To date they have resisted
attempts to move them from
their stone-built hamlets deep
in the Giant Panda Reserve

recommendations of the NCMP are intended to overcome this problem of limited population size and its attendant genetic problems by increasing the number and area of panda reserves and by translocating both people and pandas.

The NCMP proposes the designation of new panda reserves so as to incorporate as many of the remaining wild panda populations as possible. Fourteen new reserves are planned, adding an extra 424 400 hectares (over 1 million acres) of protected panda habitat to the present 6227 km^2 (2400 square miles) of panda reserves. For example, the Wolong Reserve (where most detailed panda research has been carried out) is to be linked to Fengtongzhai Reserve by the incorporation of the already established scenic reserve in Shuanghe, together with the smaller Huangshuihe and Anzihe reserves. This will effectively protect the entire panda habitat of the Qionglai Mountains. It will also ensure a steady supply of water to industry and agriculture in the Red Basin by protecting the forest cover of several water catchment areas in this region.

In Wolong around 2000 people from the Qiang minority share the reserve with the panda. As in other areas, the Qiang's agricultural activities have been a major cause of the giant panda's continuing decline. Since 1984, the Chinese government has attempted to persuade the Qiang to move further down the valley into new housing. So far the tribespeople have stayed put, continuing to work their fields and cut the forest for firewood. From the Qiang's point of view this is understandable; apart from the trauma of moving from land which may have been in a family's possession for generations, they are reluctant to lose valuable resources such as orchards and walnut trees which will take years to re-establish. The reluctance of the authorities to enforce this translocation of a whole community is due, in no small measure, to the fact that the Qiang are a minority group. The majority of Chinese belong to the Han people, and the government is very sensitive to the fears of minority groups that they could easily be swamped by the numerically superior Han. This caution in dealing with minorities even extends to the 'one family, one child' policy, introduced to stem the exponential rise in China's human population;

large families are still the norm among groups such as the Qiang.

In some cases it may be possible to redraw the reserve boundaries, swapping suitable land outside the reserve for land inside the reserve that already has a long history of human occupation. Unfortunately, this easy solution is rarely possible and translocation of the farming communities is the only option. Despite the unquestioned problems in moving settled communities from the reserve, the management plan is unequivocal. 'If we are serious about saving the pandas, there is no alternative to removing people from its last habitat, however expensive and complex that operation may prove.'[67]

That translocation is possible has been proved, admittedly on a small scale, at Tangjiahe Reserve in Sichuan Province, where sixty households numbering 300 people have been successfully resettled outside the reserve. In this case, the Forestry Department subcontracted the work of resettlement to local government officials who were paid a negotiated sum to cover all expenses and to compensate the resettled community for the inconvenience and loss of resources occasioned by the move. A similar procedure in Wolong and other areas may yet prove successful in persuading farming communities to abandon their land within the panda reserves.

If translocation of human communities poses problems, translocation of giant pandas to new areas is also fraught with difficulty. Here, the problem is not to persuade the animal to move (it is not given any say in the matter), but the creature's likely chances of survival once translocation has been forced on it. Giant pandas seem to learn the lie of their home territory, its topography, where the best resting and feeding sites are, what bamboos to eat and when to eat them, at quite a young age. Translocation will often mean releasing a panda into a different area, at a different altitudinal range, possibly with a new species of bamboo as its staple food. Can the animal relearn the arts of survival in a new area?

To date, there have been only two releases of giant panda into new locations (a third panda, the male Hua Hua, was successfully released after spending one year in captivity, but the animal was set free at its original place of capture). Zhen Zhen, an adult female, was released close to the Wolong Research Centre in the winter of 1984. She quickly travelled the 10 km (6 miles) to her previous foraging area and re-established her home range. She died there in April 1985. The release must be regarded as successful, but with one important proviso: the animal took great pains to return to her original home. Clearly, if all translocated pandas did this, the exercise would be pointless.

The second release, Xi Xi, an adult female, showed similar ranging behaviour, with the panda apparently attempting to locate her old haunts. The animal had been translocated approximately 20 km (12 miles), from Qingchuan County to Tangjiahe Reserve, both of which are in the Min Mountain range, but which have a different bamboo understorey. In this case, after spending a few days around the release site, Xi Xi moved off at speed. Assuming she was looking for her previous home range, she travelled in exactly the wrong direction. She was later found dead in very steep terrain 1200 m (4000 ft) above and many kilometres from the release point. It seems that the imperative to somehow find her way home overrode the animal's instincts to settle down and establish a new home range. Or perhaps Xi Xi, surrounded by new land and faced with different bamboo, just did not know how to cope.

So, the future for translocation must still be regarded as doubtful. In cases where the animal can get itself back to its original area, its survival chances are high. But the only attempt so far to translocate a giant panda to a truly different location has ended in failure and death. And it should be remembered that even the failed translocation was between two areas in the same mountain range. To achieve fully its potential, translocations should occur between widely spaced panda populations. The present panda distribution is subject to several

Large rivers may act as effective barriers to the movement of giant pandas, preventing isolated populations from interbreeding

irreparable breaks, and translocation is probably the most feasible of the three methods presently available to ensure gene mixing between these populations, the other two being artificial insemination and fostering of young pandas. It may be that the way forward lies in holding translocated pandas in large enclosures at their intended new home for extended periods of time, so that they can readjust slowly to the demands of their new life. This would be a costly enterprise. In any event, it will clearly be some time before pandas can be transferred between, say, Shaanxi and Sichuan Provinces with enough probability of success to make the effort involved worthwhile.

Within most panda reserves the solution to the isolation/inbreeding problem does not lie in translocation, but in simply letting the pandas do the walking. After all, during times of bamboo die-back, pandas can cover substantial distances, and may very well establish themselves in new areas, feeding on new bamboo species and meeting and mating with new partners. The problem is, of course, that pandas are now confined to small islands of forest. The solution is to build bridges, green bridges of tree and bamboo, over which the pandas can naturally migrate between isolated groups. All told, fifteen green bridges, or 'corridors', have been identified to link most of the isolated groups (see Appendix 6).

If separated panda groups can be linked by such bridges to form larger groups, they would, at a stroke, become far less vulnerable to the effects of inbreeding, genetic drift, etc. It has been calculated that only a 1 per cent exchange of genetic material per generation will be sufficient to maintain viability in most panda populations, so not many pandas need use the corridors to make the idea a success. Careful consideration has been given to the structure of these corridors. They should be located at the narrowest point between two populations, though some modification may be necessary, depending on the steepness of the terrain at that point. They must be no less than 0.5 km (about 0.3 mile) wide, though double that distance would be preferable. If necessary, the corridors should be reafforested, using native trees wherever possible, planted at intervals of not less than 5 m × 5 m, or 16 × 16 ft (too close planting crowds out bamboo). When the saplings have reached a height of 4 m (13 ft), bamboo understorey should be established beneath them, using bamboo species native to the area. No exotic bamboo planting must be allowed. Where barriers such as rivers impede the movement of pandas, artificial 'fallen logs' (around 0.5 m (18 ins) wide) should be placed across the waterway to help the panda to cross. Man-made barriers must also be regulated. In some cases simply closing a road to traffic during the hours of darkness may be enough to re-establish a panda migration pathway.

The National Conservation Management Plan is bold and imaginative – it deserves to succeed. Implementing its proposals will cost ninety-one and a half million Yuan over a five-year period, a little under ten million pounds or around two million pounds per year. Who will pay? China's resources are limited: the country is struggling to improve the standard of living of its more than one billion human inhabitants, who must be fed from agricultural land that occupies only 15 per cent of the country's total area. Given such stark facts, it is admirable that the Chinese government places such a high priority on saving the giant panda and all its wildlife. In these circumstances it is hard not to think of the millions of pounds garnered annually by the sale of toy pandas. If, just this year, a fraction of parents delayed their purchase of a toy panda and paid the cash into a panda fund, the problem of funding could be solved, and their children given a priceless gift – the continued existence in the wild of this wonderful black and white teddy-bear. Although the giant panda lives only in China, in a very real sense it belongs to the whole world. We would all be diminished by its death. And, if we can allow a creature as loved and cherished as the giant panda to vanish from the face of the earth, what hope is there for the rest of the natural world?

APPENDIX 1
NOTES ON THE TEXT

[1] Zhao, Q. and Deng, Z. 1988. Macaca thibetana at Mt. Emei, China: I A cross-sectional study of growth and development. *American Journal of Primatology* 16: 251–260

[2] Deng, Z. and Zhao, Q. 1987. Social structure in a wild group of Macaca thibetana at Mt. Emei, China. *Folia Primatologica* 49: 1–10

[3] Fox, H.M. 1949. *Abbé David's Diary*. Harvard University Press, Cambridge, Massachusetts

[4] Schaller, G.B., Hu, J., Pan, W. and Zhu, J. 1985. *The Giant Pandas of Wolong*. University of Chicago Press, Chicago

[5] *See* [4]

[6] *See* [4]

[7] *See* [3]

[8] Harkness, R. 1938. *The Lady and the Panda*. Nicholson & Watson, London

[9] Waley, A. 1918. *One Hundred and Seventy Chinese Poems*, London

[10] *See* [4]

[11] *See* [4]

[12] Janzen, D.H. 1976. *Annual Review of Ecology and Systematics* 7: 347–391

[13] *See* [12]; Chen, M.Y. 1973. Giant Timber Bamboo in Alabama. *Journal of Forestry* 71: 77; Numata, M. 1970. Conservational implications of bamboo flowering and death in Japan. *Biological Conservation* 2: 227–229; Numata, M., Ikusima, I. and Ohgo, N. 1974. Ecological aspects of bamboo flowering. Ecological studies of bamboo forests in Japan, XIII. *Botanical Magazine*, Tokyo. 87: 271–284; Petrova, L.H. 1970. Morphology of the reproductive organs of certain species of the subfamily Bambusoideae. *Botanicheskii Zhurnal* 55: 234–252

[14] Investigation Team. 1977. *Giant panda and the bamboo species in the Min Mountains*. Sichuan Forest Bureau (in Chinese)

[15] *See* [12]

[16] *See* [14]

[17] Lowrie, A.G. 1900. Effects of the late drought in the Chanda District. *Indian Forestry* 26: 503–506

[18] Munro, W. 1868. A monograph of the Bambusaceae, including descriptions of all the species. *Transactions of the Linnaean Society*, London. 26: 1–157

[19] Taylor, A.H. and Qin, Z. 1989. Structure and composition of selectively cut and uncut Abies–Tsuga forest in Wolong Natural Reserve and implications for panda conservation in China. *Biological Conservation* 47: 83–108

[20] Johnson, K.G., Schaller, G.B. and Hu, J. 1988. Comparative behaviour of red and giant pandas in the Wolong Reserve, China. *Journal of Mammalogy* 69 (3): 552–564

[21] *See* [4]

[22] Bleijenberg, M.C.K. 1984. When is a carnivore not a carnivore? When it's a panda (some notes on the nutrition of the red panda – Ailurus fulgens). Pp 23–36 in the *Red or Lesser Panda Stud Book, number 3* (A.R. Glatston ed.). Stichtung Koninklijke Rotterdamse Diergaarde, Rotterdam

[23] Davis, D. 1964. The giant panda: A morphological study of evolutionary mechanisms. *Fieldiana: Zoology Memoirs*: 1–339

[24] *See* [23]

[25] Wang Ping, Cao Chuo and Chen Maosheng. 1982. Histological survey of the alimentary tract of the giant panda. *Zoological Research* 3 (supplement): 27–28 (in Chinese)

[26] *See* [4]

[27] Moen, A. 1973. *Wildlife ecology: An analytical approach*. W.H. Freeman, San Francisco

[28] Bourlière, F. 1979. Significant parameters of environmental quality for nonhuman primates. In: *Primate ecology and human origins*, Eds I. Bernstein and E. Smith, Garland SIPM Press, New York

[29] Ruan Shiju and Yong Yange, 1983. Observations on feeding and search for the food of giant panda in the wild. *Wildlife*. 1: 5–8 (in Chinese)

[30] Yong Yange, 1981. The preliminary observations on giant panda in Foping Natural Reserve. *Wildlife*. 4: 10–16

[31] *See* [29]

[32] *See* [4]

[33] Schaller, G.B., Teng, Q., Johnson, K.G., Wang, X., Shen, H. and Hu, J. 1989. The feeding ecology of giant pandas and Asiatic black bears in the Tangjiahe Reserve, China. In: *Carnivore behaviour, ecology and evolution* (Ed. Gittlemen, J.L.). Cornell University Press, New York

[34] *See* [4]

[35] *See* [20]

[36] *See* [4]

[37] *See* [4]

[38] *See* [20]

[39] Van Soest, P. 1982. *Nutritional ecology of the ruminant*. Q and B Books, Corvallis, OR

[40] Gogan, P. 1973. Some aspects of nutrient utilisation by Burchell's Zebra Equus burchelli boehmi (Maischie) in the Serengeti–Mara region of East Africa. Master's thesis, Texas A & M University

[41] *See* [20]

[42] *See* [4]

[43] *See* [4]

[44] Kruuk, H. 1972 *The Spotted Hyena, A study of Predation and Social Behavior*, University of Chicago Press, Chicago

[45] *See* [4]

[46] Quigley, H. 1982. *Activity patterns, movement ecology and habitat utilization of black bears in the Great Smoky Mountains National Park, Tennessee*. Master's thesis, University of Tennessee; Rogers, L. 1977. *Social relationships, movements and population dynamics of black bears in northeastern Minnesota*. Doctoral thesis, University of Minnesota

[47] *See* [4]; Peters, G., Kleiman, D. and Schaller, G.B. In prep. Vocalisations of the giant panda. Quoted in [34].

[48] Yonzon, P.B. and Hunter, M.L. 1989. Ecological study of the red panda in Nepal-Himalaya. In: *Red Panda Biology*. Conference, Rotterdam, Netherlands, August 1987. (Ed. Glatston, A.R.) SPB Academic Publishers bv: The Hague, Netherlands, xv 187pp

[49] Roberts, M.S. 1981. *The reproductive biology of the red panda, Ailurus fulgens, in captivity*. Master's thesis, University of Maryland

[50] Catton, C. 1990. *Pandas*. Christopher Helm, London

[51] *See* [49]

[52] *See* [49]

[53] *See* [30]; Liu, Y. 1983. Conjectures regarding activity patterns and mating of the giant panda in winter. *Wildlife* I: 3–4; and *see* [4]

[54] Kleiman, D.G. 1983. Ethology and reproduction of captive giant pandas (Ailuropoda melanoleuca). *Zeitschrift für Tierpsychologie* 62: 1–46

[55] *See* [4]

[56] Mills, S. 1983. *BBC Wildlife* 1 (1): 8–13

[57] Roberts, M.S. and Kessler, D.S. 1979. Reproduction in red pandas, Ailurus fulgens (Carnivora: Ailuropodidae). *Journal of Zoology*, London. 188: 235–249

[58] Zhu, C. and Long, Z. 1983. The vicissitudes of the giant panda. *Acta Zoologica Sinica* 29 (1): 93–104 (in Chinese)

[59] MacKinnon, J., Bi, F., Qiu, M., Fan, C., Wang, H., Yuan, S., Tian, A. and Li, J. 1989. *National Conservation Management Plan for the Giant Panda and its Habitat: Sichuan, Gansu and Shaanxi Provinces, The People's Republic of China*. Ministry of Forestry, China. WWF, Switzerland, iv 157pp

[60] De Wulf, R., MacKinnon, J.R. and Cai, W.S. 1988. Remote sensing for wildlife management: Giant panda habitat

mapping from LANDSAT MSS images. *Geocarto International* 1988 (1): 41–50

[61] Soule, M.E. 1987. *Viable Populations for Conservation.* Cambridge University Press, Cambridge

[62] *See* [59]

[63] Princee, F.P.G. 1989. Preservation of genetic variation in the red panda population. In: *Red Panda Biology.* Conference, Rotterdam, Netherlands, August 1987. (Ed. Glatston, A.R.) SPB Academic Publishers bv: The Hague, Netherlands, xv + 187pp

[64] Glatston, A.R. In prep. Ten years after: The history of the Red Panda Studbook. In: *Proceedings of the fifth BESC meeting,*

1988. Quoted in Glatston, A.R., 1989 Demographic analysis of the red panda population. In: *Red Panda Biology.* Conference, Rotterdam, Netherlands, August 1987. (Ed. Glatston, A.R.) SPB Academic Publishers bv: The Hague, Netherlands, xv + 187pp

[65] Zwart, P. 1989. Contribution to the pathology of the red panda (Ailurus fulgens). In: *Red Panda Biology.* Conference, Rotterdam, Netherlands, August 1987. (Ed. Glatston, A.R.) SPB Academic Publishers bv: The Hague, Netherlands, xv + 187pp

[66] *See* [65]

[67] *See* [59]

APPENDIX 2
RACOON OR BEAR?

The position of the giant panda in the zoological scheme of things has been a question of sometimes fierce debate ever since its 'discovery' in 1869. Père Armand David thought that the beast he had collected in the Sichuan mountains was a bear; his friend Henri Milne-Edwards considered it a relative of the racoons, like the red panda.

The giant panda looks, superficially at least, like a bear; even internally many anatomical features, such as brain architecture, speak of an ancestry linked to the bears. The problem is that many other aspects of its detailed anatomy – for example, the structure of the teeth and the unique pseudo-thumb derived from an elongated wrist bone – link the giant panda to the red panda. Behaviourally, the giant panda has more in common with the red panda, similarities that have caused George Schaller to argue that they are closely related. The red panda is almost unanimously agreed to be a member of the *Procyonidae*, the taxonomic family containing coati mundis and racoons. So, is the bear-like giant panda in reality a monstrous racoon?

The short answer is that no one really knows. Whether a similar feature, behavioural or anatomical, indicates an evolutionary relationship or convergence is a difficult question to answer. In convergence, species from quite different lineages evolve similar structures or behaviours to deal with similar environmental conditions. Some behaviours – for example, courtship postures, scent-marking and vocalisations – remain unchanged in a variety of habitats and so are better indicators of evolutionary relationships than those which alter according to their environment. Faced with conflicting evidence of anatomy and behaviour, there seemed to be no prospect of ever achieving consensus on the evolutionary relationships of the two pandas. Were they more closely related to each other or to bears, or to racoons?

Fortunately, in the mid-1950s, molecular biology came to the rescue. Here was a way of objectively determining the pandas' ancestry, free from the subjective 'interpretive' problems which so plagued the science of anatomy (a bone can be looked at in several different ways, each observer filtering the evidence through his own prejudices and often coming up with conclusions diametrically opposed to a rival's analysis of the same bone).

As molecular biology progressed, techniques such as serum-antiserum testing, DNA hybridisation, chromosome analysis and gel electrophoresis attempted to peer into the chemical evolution of the pandas, to look for similarities with a number of members of the bear and racoon families, and to come up with a definitive answer on the nature of the pandas' relationships. The results placed the red panda firmly with the *Procyonidae*; the giant panda's genus was slightly more equivocal. Overall, most of the molecular evidence points to the giant panda as being a bear, with only a few results clouding the issue. But to draw conclusions from single features or techniques is risky: some characteristics remain unaltered over evolutionary time; others change. The least we can do is to look at as many features as possible – behavioural, anatomical and biochemical – to see if there is a recognisable trend.

If we look at the columns in Appendix 2, Figure 1, it becomes immediately obvious that the giant panda has affinities both with bears and racoons, but has more in common with the former, while the opposite is true of red pandas. It is also clear, however, that the two pandas have a great deal in common with each other, and one school of thought feels that they should even be put in the same family, the *Ailuridae*. Indeed, one evolutionary scenario imagines a small, panda-like ancestor that became adapted to eating bamboo leaves and then later gave rise to the two genera we know today. The red panda retained its ancestral diet but the giant panda added bamboo stems and, in order to cope with the tougher food, increased in size.

At the time of writing, this 'one-family' scenario is not favoured by most biologists. The overwhelming nature of the molecular evidence convinces most that the giant panda belongs with the bears and the red panda with the racoons, with any similarities between the two species being due to convergence. This seems to be the safest conclusion, but the jury is still out. Given the see-saw nature of the research to date, further studies could very well reverse the verdict. Whatever the answer, whether the giant panda is a Goliath among racoons or an aberration of the bear, it remains a remarkable example of evolutionary adaptability.

Appendix 2 Figure 1 ANATOMICAL, BEHAVIOURAL AND BIOCHEMICAL SIMILARITIES BETWEEN: GIANT PANDAS, RED PANDAS, BEARS AND RACOONS

RED PANDA

| GIANT PANDA | | | | | RED PANDA | | | |
Closer to bears	Closer to racoons	Closer to red pandas	Separate grouping	FEATURE	Separate grouping	Closer to giant pandas	Closer to racoons	Closer to bears
				Anatomical				
●	○	○		body shape		○	●	
○		○		teeth		○	○	
○				ear ossicles				
●		○		skull		○		
			○	skeleton				
		○		wrist bone				
		○		penis		○		
○	○	○		gut			○	
				Behaviour				
				REPRODUCTION				
		○		size dimorphism		○	○	
		○		oestrus and ovulation		○	○	
○		●		delayed implantation		●		○
○				weight of young at birth		○	○	
○				growth rate during lactation				
				COMMUNICATION				
○	○	○		visual signals		○	○	
○	○	○		vocal signals		○	○	
○		○		olfactory signals		○		
○				indirect visual signals				
				Biochemical				
○				immunology[1]	●			
○				gel electrophoresis[2]			○	○
○				DNA hybridisation[3]			○	
○				chromosome number[4]			○	○
○			○	chromosome banding[5]			○	○

GIANT PANDA

Code: ● stronger similarity; ○ weaker similarity

[1] Analysis of body proteins by inducing antibodies in rabbit serum. First done with albumin and transferrin in blood serum, then, in a later study, with 289 proteins. Because proteins evolve at different rates, analysis of many proteins gives a more accurate evolutionary picture

[2] Use of an electric field to separate and compare body proteins

[3] Comparison of DNA in cell nucleus; in theory, this gives a more accurate picture than protein comparisons

[4] Number of chromosome pairs in cell nucleus

[5] Pattern of heterochromatin banding in chromosomes

APPENDIX 3
FOOD

Appendix 3 Figure 1   Chemical composition (percentage of dry matter) of *S. fangiana*

Stems	All leaves	Leaves from top of stem	Leaves from bottom of stem
Crude protein 2.08	15.21	19.09	16.48
Hemicelluloses 22.90	34.93	34.59	36.93
Cellulose 45.96	27.45	25.36	21.60
Lignin 16.16	8.73	8.15	10.42
Total ash 1.86	8.75	8.75	8.77
Silica 0.42	2.32	4.52	6.45

Appendix 3 Figure 2   Plants eaten in Tangjiahe Reserve by Asiatic black bear

Species	Part eaten
Acanthopanax henryi	New stem growth, leaf
Actinidia chinensis	Fruit
Angelica sp.	Succulent stalk
Anthriscus sylvestris	Succulent stalk
Arisaema lobatum	Succulent stalk
Aster ageratoides	Leaf
Cacalia tangutica	Leaf
Caraya sp.	Fruit
Celtis biondii	Fruit
Cnidium sp.	Succulent stalk
Cornus chinensis	Fruit
Corylus sp.	Nut
Cyclobalanopsis oxyodon	Acorn
Fargesia scabrida	Shoot
Heracleum moellendorffii	Succulent stalk
Heracleum scabridum	Succulent stalk
Hydrangea sp.	New stem growth, leaf
Juglans cathayensis	Nut
Lunathyrium giraldii	Young frond
Petasites tricholobus	Leaf
Phlomis sp.	Leaf
Prunus bracyhypoda/Prunus sericea	Fruit

Figure 2—*contd*

Species	Part eaten
Quercus aliena/Quercus glandulifera	Acorns
Quercus spinosa	Acorns
Rubus coreanus	Fruit, new shoot
Salvia umbratica	Leaf

Modified from Schaller *et al* (1989), see Notes on the Text[4]

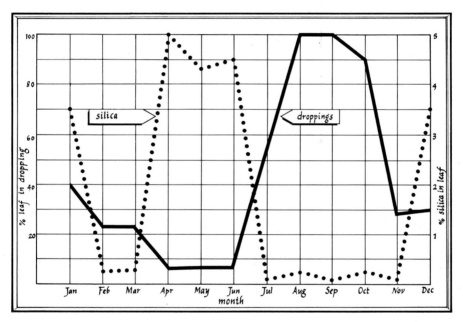

Appendix 3 Figure 3 Percentage of *Sinarundinaria* leaves in panda droppings each month compared to the average silica content of fresh leaves that month. (The June droppings were inspected only visually – not dried and weighed as in other months – and the percentage of leaf content was estimated.)
See Notes on the Text [4]

APPENDIX 4

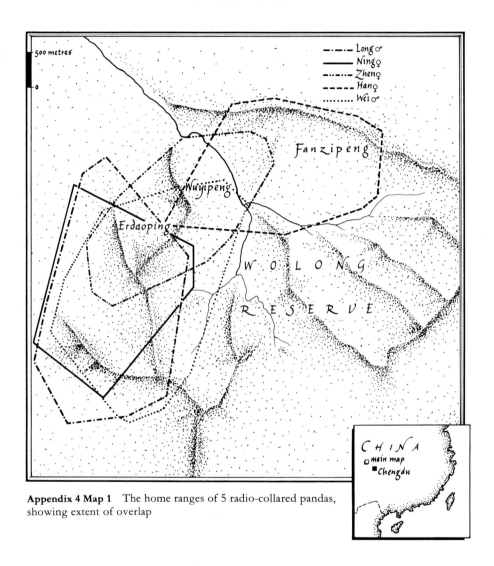

Appendix 4 Map 1 The home ranges of 5 radio-collared pandas, showing extent of overlap

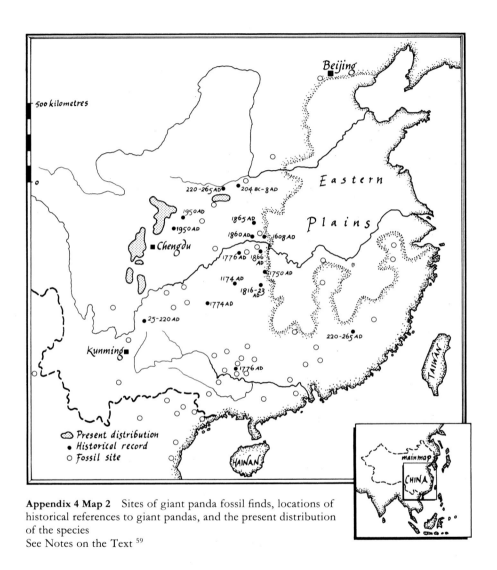

Appendix 4 Map 2 Sites of giant panda fossil finds, locations of
historical references to giant pandas, and the present distribution
of the species
See Notes on the Text [59]

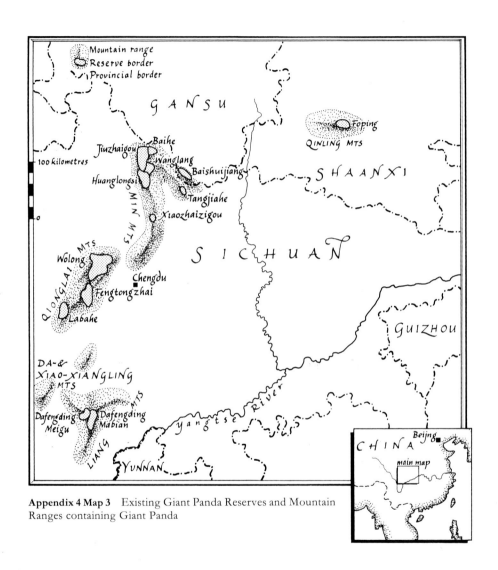

Appendix 4 Map 3 Existing Giant Panda Reserves and Mountain Ranges containing Giant Panda

APPENDIX 5
EXISTING GIANT PANDA RESERVES

Name	County	Province	Year established	Area in km^2	Estimated No of Pandas	Human residents
Foping	Foping	Shaanxi	1978	350	100	Hundreds
Baishuijiang	Wen	Gansu	1978	953	20–40	10 000
Baihe	Nanping	Sichuan	1963	200	20	0
Jiuzhaigou	Nanping	Sichuan	1978	600	40	820
Wanglang	Pingwu	Sichuan	1965	277	10–20	0
Tangjiahe	Qingchuan	Sichuan	1978	300	100–140	278
Xiaozhaizigou	Beichuan	Sichuan	1979	167	20	0
Fengtongzhai	Baoxing	Sichuan	1975	400	50	2000
Wolong	Wenchuan	Sichuan	1975	2000	130–150	3000
Labahe	Tianquan	Sichuan	1963	120	25	?
Dafengding	Mabian	Sichuan	1978	300	30–40	300-400
Dafengding	Meigu	Sichuan	1978	160	10	2000
Huanglongsi	Songpan	Sichuan	1983	400	Few	0

See Notes on the Text [59]

APPENDIX 6
PROPOSED GIANT PANDA CORRIDORS

Name	Location
Jiuzhaigou–Baihe–Wujiao	Sichuan
Majia–Caodi	Sichuan
Baima River	Sichuan
Mupi–Muzuo	Sichuan/Gansu
Qingpian	Sichuan
Caopo–Gengda	Sichuan
Pitiao–Zhenghe	Sichuan
Chongqing–Dayi–Lushan	Sichuan
Baoxing	Sichuan
Fengtongzhai	Sichuan
Meigu	Sichuan
Ebian	Sichuan
Shanlinggang	Sichuan
Shaba–Zaojiaowan	Shaanxi
Longcaoping	Shaanxi

Locations in bold specify corridors whose development should be given priority
See Notes on the Text [59]

INDEX

INDEX

Page numbers in bold type indicate illustrations